Sandra Elisabeth
Robisom D. Calado

Transforming ideas into profits:
Starting up in Brazil

1st Edition

GlobalSouth
PRESS

Published in the United States by Globalsouth Press Inc™.
All rights reserved.

Published in the United States of America

For more information, please contact info@globalsouthpress.com
or go to http://www.globalsouthpress.com/

Book design by **Héctor Guzmán**

Editing and Revising by **Marisol Alvarenga**

Transforming ideas into profits:
Starting up in Brazil

Includes bibliographical references and index.

ISBN:

978-1-943350-06-3

1. Business—Entrepreneurship
2. Entrepreneurship—Entrepreneurship Business Strategy
3. Business—Lean Start Up
4. Brazil

GlobalSouth
P R E S S

Editorial Board:

I thank my teachers who have contributed in any way with the completion of this study, and particularly my family for their support and love.

SANDRA ELISABETH

I dedicate this work to my dear wife Selma, my children Juliane and William for their support, patience and love. And my friends who always encourage me.

ROBISOM CALADO

Foreword

This book aims to provide a step by step guide for entrepreneurs to lay pen into paper, and transform them into reality.

This is not the only way to go forward, but we believe it is one strategy to be more assertive.

The book is divided in two parts: a theoretical one, which presents the main concepts to be discussed; and a practical one, which shows you how the concepts are used to effectively transform the idea in paper into the entrepreneur's venture.

The startup issue has been widely discussed. Many business magazines have questioned some entrepreneurs who develop ideas to seek investors.

Here, we will discuss how they –either fortunately or unfortunately- invest in what they will surely get results. The point to where entrepreneurs validate their ideas.

After years of crisis, especially in Brazil, some of many investors stopped their business projects and others became more selective. The important aspect to consider is that there are investment resources; the problem is the strategy you will use to prove the feasibility of your idea, other than only written in paper.

We know this might become an antagonistic debate: the entrepreneur needs money to drive his idea into action, while the investor only supplies with the money, to prove that the business is actually profitable. To this point and many times, the entrepreneur no longer needs other people's money.

Our intention with this book is to show a way to take the idea into reality, investing less resource and generating the information the market demands before investing.

You will see when entrepreneurs make use of this method in many cases, they discover their natural ability to move on sustainably with their business, and would avoid their dependence on third parties.

It is great if this is your case. You would validate your business and make it grow and develop as a company. It may even be a little slower than those who receive investments, but do not worry! The most important task is to continue "living" in the market, always through the growing line.

Have a pleasant reading!

CONTENT

Entrepreneur
en.tre.pre.ne.ur

adj (entrepreneur+neur) 1 Who achieves.2 Who ventures to
do difficult things or do things out of the ordinary; active,
audacious. sm 1 Who undertakes.2 He who takes charge of
a company (Michaelis Dictionary).

An interesting fact happened when I started writing this chapter. I set out
to start with the concept of the word "entrepreneurship" according to the
Michaelis dictionary of the Portuguese language. To my amazement, this
word did not exist. I knew I could have made an exploration in various
other sources to find what I was looking for. I decided not to do so since I
remembered a phrase from one of my elementary school teachers: "words are
not found in a dictionary because they are not so common, so we have to keep
on looking somewhere else ".

A hypothetical statement came to my mind: the word entrepreneurship is
not too common, and it is not often used in Portuguese. Yet, I don't know
whether this hypothesis is true or not, and it is not the matter of study of this
book either. What intrigued me more was that for me and the people around
me, this is a word of common use, every day and at all times.

And then another thought troubled me: are the people around me talking
about entrepreneurship and discussing this topic? Where is entrepreneurship
and how it "goes"? Why do people venture themselves? Why is there so much
material that talks about it? After so many questions, I will try to give some
answers (or new questions) on the subject.

1.1 Entrepreneurship and its historical background

There are several theories and several books that deal with the origins of entrepreneurship and the paths taken by entrepreneurs. I commit myself here to just go over the history of entrepreneurship slightly, since this issue would enable us to write another book.

Rereading the meaning of the word entrepreneur "who ventures to do difficult things or do things out of the ordinary", I venture to say that man always has achieved his goals since the beginning of times, and that if he did not do so, it would not be necessary to either read (or write) this book.

Thus, the cave man who created the fire, the wheel, the one who learned to plant and hunt was an entrepreneur. He did not "sell" the fire service to others just because he needed to, but he surely taught his children and grandchildren. Due to this exchange knowledge, he got the possibility of a long life.

This man has evolved, created cities, armies to protect their cities, made trades to feed people; and in the process he got to mercantilism and to the wake of capitalism. Recalling the story, it was at this time when the Industrial Revolution started and the entrepreneur figure appeared with those "enterprise" features we know nowadays.

So far it is clear that entrepreneurship and the entrepreneur always existed, it is all a matter of nomenclature. It is relevant to keep in mind that the entrepreneur is the one who performs difficult tasks, who undertakes projects and stands out of the ordinary.

Without any doubt, individuals can also be entrepreneurs at their workplaces, in the company context where they work . In fact and for sure, you can be a very successful entrepreneur.

1.2 Reasons to achieve

Each entrepreneur has a unique and own reason to undertake a project, a dream to achieve. This is an inner need in every human being.

Unfortunately we are simplistic and lack the ability to externalize theoretically –as we do in writing- all these motives to start a business or project. Therefore, an entrepreneur ventures moved by necessity, and not necessarily by opportunity.

1.2.1 Entrepreneurship by necessity

The entrepreneur by necessity is one that does not exactly choose to undertake. Life and job circumstances make him/her start a business somehow. Due to this urgency, an entrepreneur cannot always measure the value given to the customer, who is surely a client, the one who will finance this business.

We cannot generalize that the bricklayer, the painter, a manicure working at home —to mention some- have become entrepreneurs out of necessity. Many of these professionals effectively saw an opportunity to make money and would continue with that profession. For instance, my father was a bricklayer all his life, and like every entrepreneur he had ups and downs, but he made the choice because in the city where we lived in the 60s, there were no professionals in this area.

In the 90s I saw many braking points at the market opening, as well as many former employees of these industries (with advanced age for the labor market, who only knew about fabrics, etc). That moved me to undertake in the industry of making clothes by necessity in the same region. Today, there is considerable growth and success in the area. Nevertheless, there are some others that ended up closing their doors soon in the early years.

That is, the need to earn money through entrepreneurship always speaks louder than understanding the market and clients. Then we are referring to that entrepreneurship by need.

1.2.2 Entrepreneurship by opportunity

The one who already ventures by opportunity sees a gap in the market, an open space that neither a person nor a company can fulfill. It could be a completely innovative business or not. Philip Kotler and Steve Blank explain that we can find an opportunity in the market in different ways:

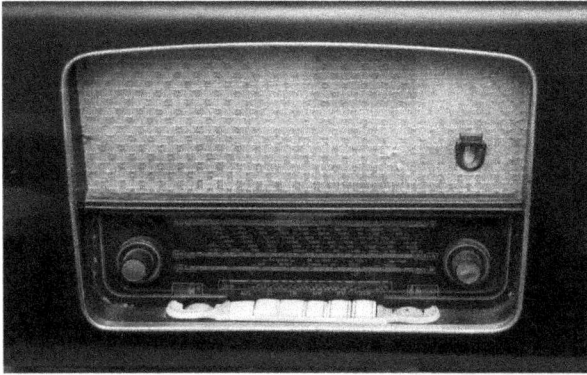

- A new product in a market that does not yet exist, for example as when the radio was invented. The product radio did not exist and neither had we known public profile would effectively buy this unit and would listen to news instead of reading them.

- A new product for an existing market, for example when Google Maps was created. The people, the market, were using printed maps to locate, for which they had to pay. After the creation of Google Maps, they continued using maps, but now online on the Internet, and without having to pay anything.

- A product that already exists in a new market, for example in new neighborhoods there are opportunities to begin trades already known, though nonexistent in that market, such as bakeries, butcher shops, newsstands, schools, to mention some.

How do we realize market opportunities? Observing customers (your target audience), and developing that special thing that would meet their needs and desires. If you realize your audience likes fresh and warm bread and there is no bakery nearby to offer this product, you have an opportunity.

If your client has limited time to go to stores, you have the opportunity to sell online. Or even, if your target audience has neither time to shop in stores nor access to Internet, then here you have another chance to bring them the products.

I know I have presented some logical facts, but it is only with the purpose to exemplify as quickly and simply as possible. It is each entrepreneur's decision to identify existing opportunities that yet nobody has noticed. Which customers have not been served properly? Who are the individuals that have made their adjustment to companies possible due to the companies' incapacity to make them adapt?

Entrepreneurs who analyze these factors are those who embark for an opportunity. Observe that I have not mentioned business model, feasibility analysis, etc. This is because both, the entrepreneur by necessity as well as the entrepreneur by opportunity, prepare themselves after defining what they will do. The difference consists in who discovers the real market opportunity, and who ventures after being pushed by the context to do so.

1.3 Difficulties encountered by entrepreneurs

According to the Brazilian Service of Support for Micro and Small Enterprises (SEBRAE), only about 70% of new businesses closes before completing their first year of life in Brazil. The Global Entrepreneurship Monitor data (GEM) does not differ, and shows the ratio is approximately 60% worldwide.

Now, if we talk of high-tech business, the percentage of companies that close before completing its first year is 90%, according to a survey in Silicon Valley with over 12,000 companies in 2011 (Hermann, 2011).

Many difficulties have been found by entrepreneurs who end up showing an early mortality of their business, being among those the lack of credit facilities for the amateur entrepreneurs, the economic and social crisis of the country where they live, or even no family and friends support. The difficulties are numerous and there is still a lot to write about this issue. However, we will focus on the already identified as the main reasons for businesses to close at an early stage. This research was carried out by three different entities - SEBRAE, 2013; GEM, 2010; Hermann, 2011 (notice they are all studies from different years and countries, though the same results).

"One of the main reasons for discontinuing startups is the internal management problem or problems related to understanding the real needs of the market, and the interpretation of available opportunities."

In other words, entrepreneurs (even those who venture by opportunity) cannot either see the opportunities in the market, nor even validate their idea. Therefore they would close their doors earlier than expected. This is indeed the most difficult part people face when taking the decision to venture these days.

1.4 Is every entrepreneur the "owner" of a startup?

Here comes the question: is every entrepreneur the "owner" of a startup? To give an answer we must first understand what a startup is. Let us see some concepts:

Acs and Amorós (2008), claim that a startup is "the process of creating a growing business," that is, any business company within the initiation process would be considered a startup.

Other researchers disagree with Acs and Amorós, and define startup according to the age of the company, considering from a newly formed company to one with 8 or 10 years.

Elfring and Hulsink (2007) cited by Brigidi (2009) deals startups under their categories: independent, spin-offs and incubated. Startups are independent companies that undertake their businesses on their own, "alone"; Spin-offs are the union of two or more startups that are acting in different activities and come together to meet the same market; and the incubated ones are those that start their business within a non-profit organization aiming to monitor and develop the startup. In Brazil there are governmental incubators maintained by universities or business institutions such as SEBRAE (SEBRAE, 2012).

Synthesizing the concept of startup, Ries (2012) has defined it as an "designed institution to create new products and services under conditions of extreme uncertainty", in or out of a large company.

Ries (2012) completes this definition adding that a startup´s ultimate goal is to find the right element to create. In other words, to discover what customers want and how much they will pay to have it, as quickly as possible and without any potential of losing.

Based on the concept of startup presented by Ries (2012), we can say that an entrepreneur not always owns a startup. This is to say that if today I decide to open a franchise, the prospect degree of uncertainty in this endeavor would be very low: the franchisor (when serious) will provide the market financial aspects, will point out at the opportunities where I am installing the franchise, and how and when I will receive upon my investment. Now, if I create a new product or service (it could be within this same franchise), which has not been tested on the market, then I will have created a startup.

Thus, some employees of companies could be startup entrepreneur owners without necessarily having a membership in a company.

This concept changes everything we knew so far about managing enterprises; it indicates that even an established business in the market will have along its lifetime, many commencements as well as startups... and nowadays to survive they really need to always innovate (create startups).

You have read the main concepts of startups, but what exactly is a scenario? Shall we find out?

Scenario
sce.na.rio

sm (wide scenario) **1** set of scenes and views appropriate to the facts that are represented.**2** sequence of scenes in the cinema or theater.**3** Panorama.**4** A place where facts happen (Michaelis Dictionary).

Our goal in this chapter will be to present an overall collection of scenes where the facts will be related to the development of projects of very high uncertainty; nowadays known as the startups scenario.

2.1 Incubators x accelerators

We have always heard that an entrepreneur needs to seek partners and people as aides in the difficult journey to undertake any project. As a recommendation, I encourage you to look for incubators and accelerators. But what are these? Are they the same thing? If not, what are the differences?

In Brazil, a business incubator is almost always linked to an educational institution, a public body or to a class of entity (SEBRAE, FIESP, and CIESP, among others). This individual aims to support the development of micro and small businesses, depending on the incubator for a period of 2 to 4 years.

This support can be materialized through training, courses, consulting, technology support and mainly work space; this is because the incubators offer a place for micro and small businesses that are starting to settle at a very low price when compared to the stalls of rentals´ costs in the market.

The focus of the incubators is still the product development or services to meet the market. An entrepreneur seeks to get his project accepted into the incubator needs. First, the business plan is presented and aims to demonstrate the product can generate profits. There is no need to show something unique and extravagant, or to be extremely innovative. There is only the need to be a good product or service.

And every year, when a company is out of the incubator, the incubators notice by inviting micro and small entrepreneurs to participate in their selection process.

Photo 01: A business incubator

In other words, accelerators have a slightly different concept: they, as well as incubators, assist entrepreneurs in developing their business, but unlike the incubators, they are not concerned with the final product, but rather in the identification of the customer´s values. Thus, the main activity of the accelerator is rather to make customers grow instead of the products. Let me explain:

Incubators hatch micro and small companies, the accelerator expedites startups. We have seen in the previous chapter that a startup is a small company, but not all micro companies are startups. (Now there is a meaningful difference between accelerator and incubator, though it is not my explanation).

The main objective of the accelerator is to assist the entrepreneur in the discovery of "making money out of the ascertained opportunity." It is not necessarily the product by itself, but the recently found opportunity. Thus, a startup first identifies who your customers are and what they need or would like to receive; then it determines that the product or service to be delivered meets the customer's needs.

It seems like something out of this world, but that is how startups think (or should think), because as Eric Ries and Steve Blank says, "it does not help to create the best product in the world, to patent it so no one can copy it, otherwise you will have nobody to sell to, and nobody to buy. "

This is so true. If we take a look at the list of patented products with the X list of products effectively made by their creators to make money; I did not mean they would get rich, but they would be able to live out of what they have created.

This is another interesting difference, the accelerator prefers products that are not patented, and services with no record. When the patent is made, there is no immediate way of making changes or adjustments to the product; everything will have to be sent to the registry patent for the patent to come with the product, and if the accelerator's goal is quicken this process will not be fast.

And speaking of time, an accelerator begins and ends its process within 1 year, enough time for the entrepreneur to fulfill some tasks: find a client, create a minimum viable product, test it on the market and make the pivots needed to measure the business viability, whether you have customers or not, or even the acceptance or non-acceptance of the market. This does not mean one would get rich in one year, but whether it would be worth or not to continue investing in the business.

The biggest accelerator benefit is the fact that when mentors differ from consultants, they do not say what the entrepreneur should do, but they do show them scenarios, possibilities and make them think about what decision to make. I (the author) do not particularly like the traditional consultancies where the consultant presents when and how it has to be done. Why should I do it the way the consultant wants and not my way? Is my approach not fast enough? In the accelerators´ companies, the mentors have the role of talking with startups, of showing the taken paths, which of those went wrong and which did not , of leaving the entrepreneurs think about "what to do" and "how." This strategy will allow entrepreneurs have the expertise to make decisions. Relying on consultants to know what to do will no longer be necessary.

Photo 02: Accelerator companies

In any case, the important thing is to identify what your need is, the path that you want to follow. Talk to people, meet incubators and accelerators that can help you, but get with the partners that will only help you!

2.1.1 National Program for Startups Business Acceleration in Brazil - Startup Brazil[1]

The Start-UP program starts in Brazil in 2012 to speed up startups in the country. For this, they support projects in the IT area, whose characteristics are to be innovators and aides for the national development.

It is an initiative of the Brazilian federal government, created by the Ministry of Science, Technology and Innovation (MCTI) in partnership with accelerators to support the growing technology companies, startups, and those having Softex as operational manager.

The Start-up Brazil is part of the Greater IT, Strategic Program for Software and IT Services, which in turn is one of the actions of the National Strategy for Science, Technology and Innovation (ENCTI), which chooses ICTs among the crucial programs to boost the Brazilian economy.

How does the Startup Brazil program work?

The program works by one-year duration issues. For each edition there is a release of two public calls, one to qualify and enable accelerators, and the other to select startups with semiannual rounds.

After the accelerators and startups have been chosen in the program, the acceleration process can start. At this point, startups have access to up to US $ 200,000 in research and development for their professionals, and the possibility to participate in a series of events and activities sponsored by the program for training and approach customers as well as investors, and the International Hub in Silicon Valley / USA. Moreover, startups receive investments of acceleration and have access to services such as infrastructure, mentors and training in exchange of participation percentage. In addition to the accelerators, companies are also partnered with the health authority.

---

1 Information collected at the program website: www.startupbrasil.org.br/programa/

The chart below shows how the Brazil Startup works:

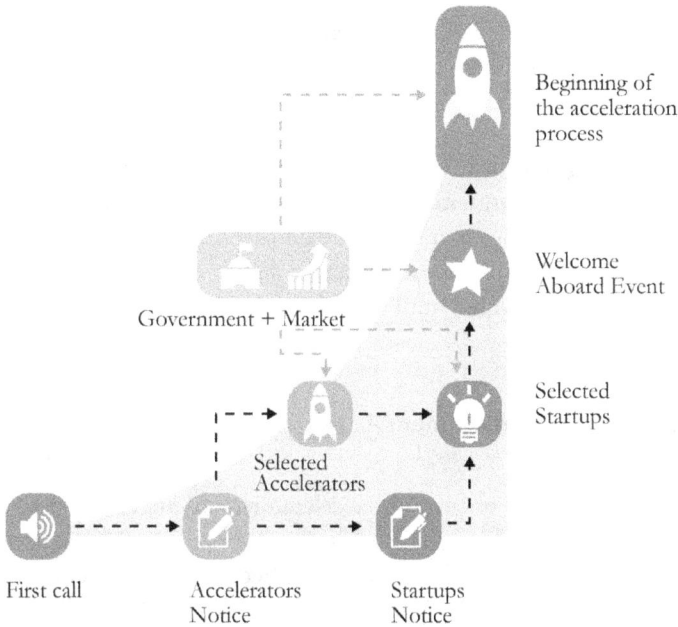

Who can participate in the Startup Brazil?

Every year the Startup Brazil opens an edition for the Startups selections. In 2014, there were 100 vacancies open for technology startups, being 75% of the vacancies for the Brazilian entrepreneurs and 25% intended for international entrepreneurs.

Four-year constituted startups could apply to develop software or hardware solutions. They should suggest some accelerators among those who participate in the Startup Brazil.

But most importantly, the startups that already received investment from one of the program participant accelerators cannot participate in Startup Brazil.

Another interesting point is that Brazilians living abroad for more than three years can also apply as international startups, and compete only with others who have registered under this category.

Now, it is very significant to read the notices and be aware of the changes. In the past, when the program was launched there was a year in which there were no changes on the operative modalities of the program. This was understandable because the Startup Brazil is also a 'startup' and like any new business, needs to be pivoted until it reaches 'perfection'.

2.2 Love Money and Investment Angel

In Brazil the movement of startups, accelerators, and angel investors is very new. In fact, this movement is still a Startup in Brazil. In 2011, a non-profit institution called Angels of Brazil was launched to assist the entrepreneurs and investors to better understand this scenario.

Angels of Brazil states that an angel investor is the investment made by individuals with their own capital in start-ups with high growth potential (*startups*). That is, people who have cash invest in startups, instead of investing in savings in the stock market in the CBD.

Notice that INVESTMENT is not a synonym for loan or finance - the startup does not have to return the money that was placed on business; so little is loan or financing repayable (that money we get to undergo with a project and then it just pays the bills). Investors want financial return from what is invested, they want to apply 10 and later earn 20, as when we put our money in savings or buy stocks.

Of course, every investment involves risks, so it is not a loan. The angel investor becomes a member of the business and assumes the risk of not receiving anything in return, as well as when investing in the stock market.

Because of the risk of losing money on the deal, usually Angel Investors in Brazil are executives, professionals, successful entrepreneurs, former executives of large industries, people who have a capital or financial reserves to invest; they become a minority shareholders of the business, and where they have no executive position at a startup (they don´t make the final decisions), but they go along with the entrepreneurs and provide them mentoring.

In fact, what you receive from Angel Investment is not the money itself, pure and simple; but the opportunity to receive mentoring from more experienced people, who have had their business, and to develop networking in favor of the startup's growth.

And what is Love Money? It is simply the chance that a person´s family gives him or her to be without a steady job to develop business. That's right, when an entrepreneur decides to invest at all times in business and having no income of his or her own, someone else will have to at least support for a period. This is your first investor.

See what the Angels of Brazil say about Love Money:

It is the investment made by family and friends, a company stage where just a friendship or family relationship justifies a financial incentive. In general, this contribution is to help in taking the company's role and keep the first months of life.

Generally, angel investors make contributions from 50 to 500 thousand reals and Love Money and the values are up to 50 thousand. The important thing is to understand that in the case of startups only money means nothing, the risks of venturing are many and seeking partners who can help to minimize this risk is much more than 1 million. This is what an investor said when I spoke in a DemoDay: "if today I give you $1 million as an investment in your business, what would you do? How will that money turn into 2 or 3 million?" See how mentoring is more important than money alone?

2.3 What accelerators and investors are looking for?

It is true that when we talk about angel investment or accelerator, there is always someone who says, if there is some money left, then they are good projects. So far we are doing great, but what is considered a good project? What does it need to be or have to be classified as such?

In this chapter, we will present some accelerator tips and many investors' strategies on how they do it.

2.3.1 Accelerator tips

Minimum prerequisites (this is the minimum to be expected):

Team: it is important to have a cohesive and multidisciplinary team, that is, there is no point for anybody to do the same thing. A company is made of people who complement each other, so when reaching out to members do not forget: they need to complement their knowledge.

There is no use of hiring out, the accelerators prefer business where the main team consists on business partners. Who ensures you that your employee will not learn everything with you and then go find another job? This is normal, wise and should be done. So for you not to get angry and have to spend time with someone new all over again is better to split the gains and losses with a partner.

Innovation: the product you are developing needs to be innovative. Startup = uncertainty –Do you remember I mentioned this before? Yes, that's right.

Without innovation there is no reason to invest time and mentoring in any project. For instance, if you want to open a "Mc Donald´s copy" okay, you can and you can even get rich with this. However, there is something wrong: just copy what the Mc Donald´s is now, the recipe is already ready. If you were be able to compete with it, there is enough discussion for another book and then not all the mentoring of the world would help you, unless you decide to do a fast food restaurant with something different and innovative.

What is innovation? We have several different concepts for innovation, but I would like to paraphrase Steve Blank and think that what he says is the basis for innovation, "to develop a customer, find out what the customer needs or wants that himself does not know yet; it may be from a differentiated service to a disruptive product (non existing) ..." That to me is innovation, something new that no one has ever done yet.

Scale: good if you have the best team in the world and the most innovative product, now we need to know if what you do is scalable, that is, if it can raise sales. The fixed cost will not increase at all and the variable cost will move very little. What this means in practice is that if you can create a software, for example, copy 01 you will have the fixed cost and have a high variable cost, as is the entire development, research, innovation, etc. Now when producing the software 1,000th it won´t have more development costs, research, innovation; I'm just making a copy on a CD and selling it. I will only have the material cost.

In addition to the costs involved, we must also understand the product/service that can be easily replicated without you having to be in several places at the same time for this to happen.

If your product has these characteristics, it is replicable, congratulations! If not, great, you make money with it but don´t expect it to become the next Google right away.

Scope of business: many entrepreneurs do not realize that each accelerator specializes in a different area of expertise, mainly due to their origin and their mentors. There are accelerators that only accept projects of Information Technology; others, specific sectors such as Creative Economy. So, before sending a request for acceleration read the accelerator information, there is nothing worse than receiving a negative answer only because you lack reading.

IMPORTANT: Even if your product is amazing, and if the accelerator has no knowledge about it, they will not tell you! Be aware!

Does it cost anything?

First, if you think it is a "cost", then stop your business now and start writing your resume. This is investment. Investment in your business, in your product, in you.

Each accelerator works in a different way, it is for the entrepreneur to identify which accelerator combines more with the product and the way of thinking. That said, I present some possible ways:

<u>1st Fixed Investment from the entrepreneur +% of sales of a short period:</u>

In this way the Accelerator asks for a fixed monthly investment by the entrepreneur in the accelerator during the period in which the MVP (Minimum Viable Product) is being developed. By the end of this period, sales are beginning with a % that is billed to the accelerator ranging from 1 to 10%, depending on the deal.

2nd participation in society:

Here the accelerator becomes a partner in business with a share of 5% to 20% over a period of usually 5 years. This means that if a large group of angel investors commit in your business, part of that money goes to the accelerator.

3rd pitches:

Many accelerators also charge the pitches, i.e. the presentation that you will give them of your projects. On that day, they bring investors and other accelerators to assess your business, increasing its visibility. If you do well on the pitch, probably you will still have to do one of the first two investment models aforementioned in the accelerator.

Anyway, in every way the accelerator only wins when the entrepreneur wins, in the first model, if it does not sell, the accelerator gets nothing unless the coverage of fixed costs and the second model, the accelerator gets nothing and can still lose a lot; therefore, so many of them begin to charge the pitch when using this modality.

2.3.2 Angel Investor Tips

Minimum prerequisites:

1st Staff: again we speak of team; angel investors seek the same team features than the accelerator.

2nd Business Model: How will you make money with your project? This is basically the question, and do not try to answer it with "advertisements" - then your project will already be out (why someone will announce his or her products and services with rather than with Google or Facebook? – some words from various investors that we spoke with), think more about these words and then ask how you can make money even with the project.

3rd Minimum Viable Product: Is your MVP ready? Have you tried it on the market? Have some customers already bought your product? If the answer is yes, great! If not, why? You can't produce it to deliver by lack of money, you could not deliver because of lack of money. If the answer is none of these, then make your MVP and go sell it and get feedback. You will need to show this to angel investors.

4th Return Forecast: How much have you sold? What is the forecast return of your business? This is not a typical question of American angel investors, but the Brazilian. We acquire little risk, so this information becomes important. Notice that no one is talking of millions, the account is simple: I spent R $ 500.00 to start a business last month, this month I already have R $ 575.00 in return. Great 15% in return on investment!

5th Innovation: Again innovation! The same concept, the same queries that the accelerators and the angel investors do.

6th Scale: Your business needs to have scale. Remember, S C A L E.

7th and MOST IMPORTANT: SYNERGY: there has to be synergy between the entrepreneur and angel investor. The angel investment is like a "marriage" on both sides, you can't get married without having synergy!

Mark Barcelos in 2014 presented the results of his research on this marriage between Investor and Entrepreneur. Below we present a summary view of his work.

HOW VENTURE CAPITALISTS AND THE BRAZILIANS STARTUPS DECIDE TO "GET MARRY"	
VENTURE CAPITAL	**STARTUPS**
Do deep analysis on :	The entrepreneurs get support on:
-Market	-Investor experience
-Business model	-Intellectual contribution;
-Risks	-Creation of Strategic contacts;
-Entrepreneurs profile backing up the business	-Business experience exchange

Other tips:

-Master what they are doing:

> Know all the market variables deeply;
> Have the figures in this market;
> Know exactly how you will make money from it.

- Show the attractiveness of your project - what problem does it solve in the value chain?

-When you do not know all the answers be HUMBLE and say, I can't answer that!

-The entrepreneur must have clear solutions to help the world, investors and himself. When it becomes clear that the entrepreneur just wants the investors' money, the relationship turns bad.

-Ability to listen to the tips of investors with the purpose of improving the project.

CHAPTER 03
WHERE DOES THE LEAN METHODOLOGY COME FROM?

In the previous chapters we briefly present what entrepreneurship is, and current startups´ scenarios. Now we will talk a little bit more about the Lean methodology that has been used by large worldwide companies in order to reduce waste and improve return.

Before we actually begin the subject, let us understand what methodology is:

Methodology
me.tho.do.lo.gy

sf (method [2] + logo2 +gy 1) 1 Scientific study of the methods.2 Art of guiding or the spirit of the search for truth.3 Filos Part of the logic that deals with reasoning methods, as opposed to formal logic.M. Teaching: theory of teaching procedures, general or particular to each discipline; theoretical teaching (Michaellis Dictionary).

Despite the apparent difficulty in understanding what methodology is, let's look at the following meanings: "art of guiding or the spirit in the search for truth"; i.e. a logical way to get a result and that when repeated (the logical form) would generate a result the same way as mentioned before. Simple comparison example, to draw a travel route, a path that leads us to the arrival point. If in the next journey we use the same route, we arrive to the same place. It is to get to the same place (success, for example) that we use a strategic methodology.

3.1 Lean History

Lean, as a working method emerged in the 50´s with Toyota and Ohno, but it only became known between the 70´s and 80´s. Initially it was called Japanese Model of Production and was later known as the Toyota Production. After studies were made of Japan's success in his new way of working, without waste, ensuring a minimum inventory and a different pace; it was believed that it would not be replicated in the West what was done in the East. But between 1980 and 1990 Toyota showed that the results were not due to geographical and cultural issues, but to the method of issues. During this period, General Motors and Toyota had joined Nummi (New United Motor Manufacturing) and soon this factory (known as the least productive unit GM) became an exemplary unit of automobile manufacturing in the US, thus proving that the theories related to Japanese culture and geography were wrong.

Toyota Manuals were the first to list the main waste: wasted time with concerting or refusing, production beyond the necessary or before the required time, unnecessary operations in the manufacturing process, transportation, stock, human movement and waits. Its main elements and the basis for the company were participation, productivity and quality.

This working method was improved and is now presented from manufacturing to the creation of startups. We call this Lean work philosophy: producing without wasting, thus increasing the return on investment.

3.2 Diversification of Lean: Lean Service; Lean Healthcare to the Lean Startup

As previously seen the lean method was born in the Toyota Company and was completely focused on the production and for the factory floor. After a period of time this methodology began to be used in all organizational areas.

This is because the lean drives the reduction of *lead time* and waste disposal. Womack (1996), Ohno (1997) Liker (2009) state that lean is a management philosophy focused on adding value, improving the quality of products and services by reducing the eight types of waste, which are: over-production lead time, transportation, excess processing, inventory, motion, defects and not using people's creativity.

These eight wastes (basically, the eight wastes mostly studied) happen in any public or private organization, in the development of products, services, or commerce, management or on the factory floor.

Thus, one of the major goals of the *lean* philosophy, is therefore to reduce the costs of a company the most - extinguishing any kind of waste - and increasing profitability - providing greater value to products and developed services.

Based on lean manufacturing, the Lean Thinking has been developed. *Lean Thinking,* is according to Murman E. (2002) the dynamic knowledge-based and focused on the client process, through which all people in a defined company, continuously dispose of waste in order to create value.

In medicine we also have the *Lean Healthcare,* in order to enhance patients and employees, increasing the quality and minimizing waste (LIKER, JK; HOSEUS, M., 2009; Murman, E.; et al., 2002).

Here is a short timeline to understand how the lean methodology has spread and is now applied in all sectors:

1950 - Japanese Production System

1970 - Toyota Production System

1988 - Lean Production - Lean Manufacturing

1990 - Lean Construction

2003 - Lean Office

2003 - Lean Education

2013 - Lean Accounting

2005 - Lean Service

2006 - Lean Healthcare

2010 - Lean IT / Lean Agile

2010 - Lean Startup

3.3 Knowing a little bit more about Lean

Before we talk about lean itself, it is important to understand that when we speak of this subject, one should speak of competitive advantage, pulled and pushed systems, supply management, project management, product development, teamwork, preventing defects, standardization and continuous improvement.

So, we will start our discussions about lean going briefly through each of the previous items.

3.3.1 Competitive Advantage

With his *marketing* and logistics vision, Christopher (2007), believes that market success is related to competitive advantage and to the three Cs: company, competitors and customers. It should be obtained the advantage to the customer at the cost he is willing to pay, i.e. cost and value advantage, in which the value advantage is to be reliable and responsive with personalized services. The cost advantage is to have synchronized supply, asset turnover and management capacity, using the appropriate ability. According to him the support and primary activities should be organized by matrix and sequential manner to achieve the desired profit margin for business continuity, as shown in the figure below:

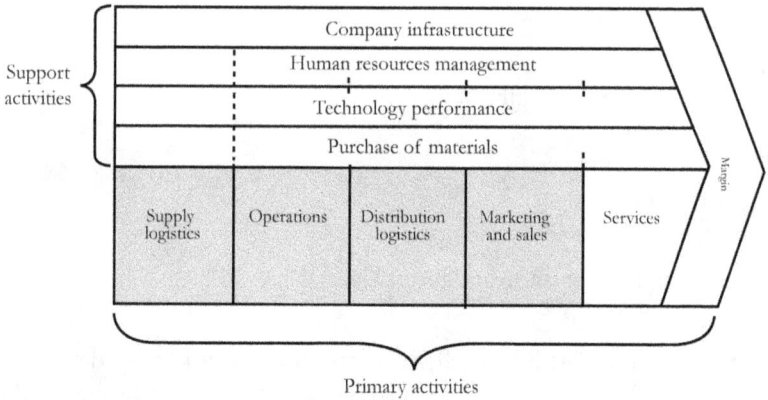

Figure 01: Value chain (Porter, 1985 *cited in* Christopher, 2007)

The competitive advantage today is the effective management of time, as Daugherty and Pittman (1995) said that it should be used strategies based on time throughout the distribution, from production to point of sale, as when delivery does not meet the needs of customers lost opportunities arise and, without a process of rapid manufacturing, the advantages diminish even more to the point of leaving a space that can be filled by the old or new competitors. The company needs to achieve good levels of responsiveness upstream and downstream throughout the supply chain with greater flexibility and agility (REICHHART; Holweg, 2007).

3.3.2 Pulled and pushed Systems

In the pushed production system (Figure 2), which is classified as traditional, the materials are moved to the next stage as soon as they are processed, usually in large lots with long *lead times. Faced with so much material processing, administration is not easy. Management is then induced to act in a corrective manner. Seeking the use of manufacturing capacity and the largest volume of production, the productive surplus stocks is when you achieve your goals.*

Usually there´s a difficulty in achieving the mix, that is, serving the customer. The problems are not visible and difficult to solve. The flow interruptions are more constant and the final quality as well as the costs are not as competitive globally.

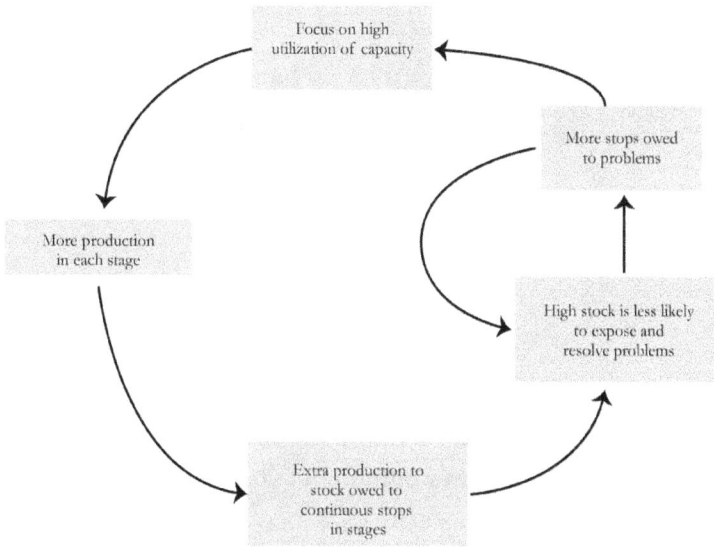

Figure 02: *(* **SLACK** *et al.,* **2009) Analogy of pushed production**

In pull production system, which ranks as lean, the materials are moved only when the next step calls, usually in small batches with shorter lead times than in the traditional system, facilitating the management of the supply chain value stream. The flow manager makes the chain mapping and strives for perfection, trying to act preventively. His biggest concern is to produce only the needs of the client, with assured quality, avoiding interruptions of the production process, as shown in Figure 03 (Slack et al., 2009).

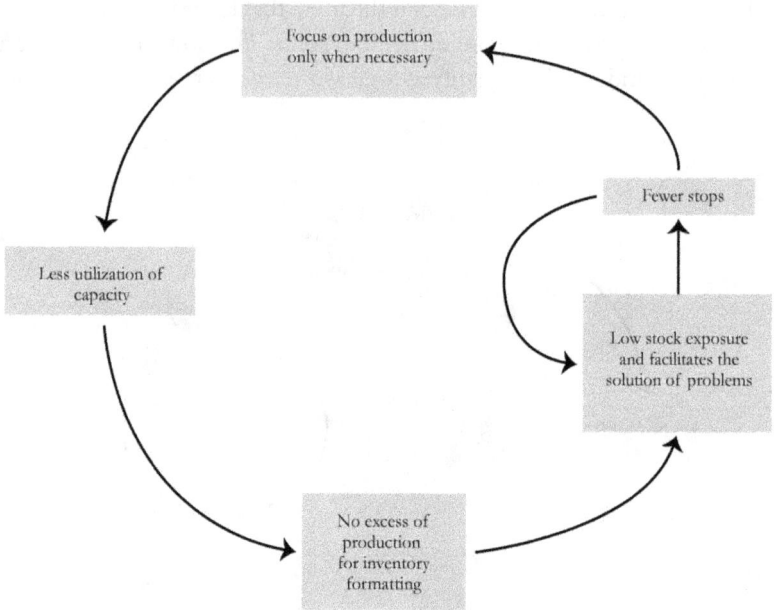

Figure 03: Analogy of pull production (Slack *et al.*, 2009)

It is understood that manufacturing is born from a project, with operational requirements to serve customers based on parameters, and whose structure is not rigid, but evolves continuously.

3.3.3 Supply Management

The flow value is any action with or without aggregate value which is required for the transformation of each product, where it is important the production flow from raw materials to the consumer, and the conception flow until its release. The total flow goes through the entire value chain, towards the consumer and starts at the last supplier layer and runs through the manufacturing. Figure 4 shows it as follows.

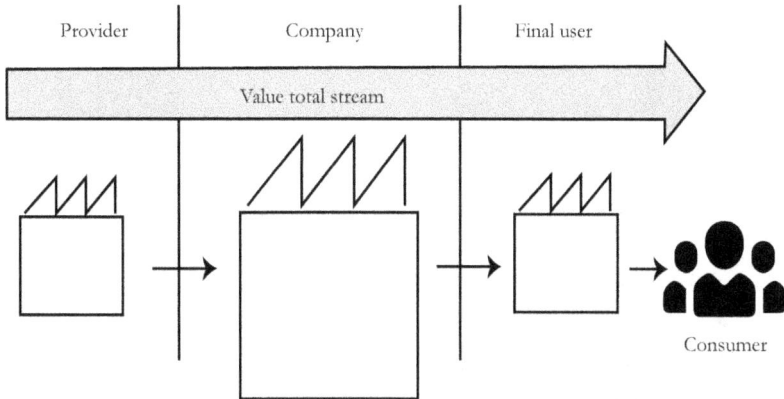

Figure 04: Illustration of total flow value (adapted Rother; SHOOK, 1998).

There is already awareness among the manufacturing companies that at managing the supply chain have strong strategic implications and, through it, you can increase competitiveness. However, there has emerged over the appreciation of the flow of products and / or services, and information flow, that in the last two decades companies have gradually applied the mapping tool of the value chain.

Value chain or supply chain is the network of services, materials and information flows that connect the customer relationship processes, order fulfillment and relationship with the company's suppliers and their suppliers and customers (Krajewski et al., 2009).

Managing the supply chain is to manage relations from the upstream (from the beginning) and the downstream (to the end) with suppliers and customers to deliver more value to customer at a lower cost to the supply chain as a whole. It is a network of connected and interdependent organizations (Figure 05), working together in mutual cooperation and arrangements, to control, manage and improve the flow of raw materials and information from suppliers to final customers (Christopher, 2007).

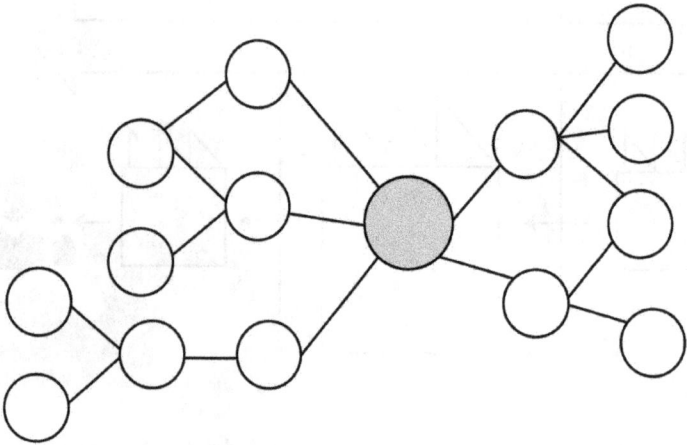

Figure 05: The supply network (Christopher, 2007).

In the center of the supply network there is the enterprise (focal company), and companies B and C (focal level) are related companies or even competitors. To the right of the graphic the *output*, customers by layers or also called customer by line , to the left there is the *input*, suppliers by layers or line. When it comes to the prospect that the chain is being designed, it has the company A left, the upstream, the layers of suppliers and to the right of Company A, the downstream, are the layers of customers . In the illustration, the direction flow of goods and / or services goes from left to right and the information flow in the opposite direction. In dotted lines always from right to left, there are the stimuli for the supply. The direction indicates what you want to achieve or where you want to walk (CARVALHO; PALLADINI, 2005).

3.3.4 Project Management

Project Management is understood to be all of leadership and organization-method tasks required for the development of a successful design. Slack et al. (2009), Correa and Correa (2007) and Murman et al. (2002) pointed out that the project management should include activities for goal setting, organization, planning, execution, control and monitoring of all tasks and resources needed to achieve the objectives defined for a project.

A project is an undertaking in which during a certain period of time, it should reached a defined goal and characterized as essentially a single effort . The tools of project management method are described and used in the guidelines: planning guidelines, resource and time planning , and risk and escalation management. It is often applicable in development, manufacturing and quality management (PRADO, 2004a; PRADO, 2004b, OAK; Rabechini JR, 2008; XAVIER, 2009).

The resource and time planning means the resources available for the required work packages to efficiently achieve the objectives and defined milestones. Eventually, objectives, milestones, work packages or resources need to be adjusted to achieve optimal overall situation. Therefore, it becomes important to maintain the project goals and deadlines, it avoids multiple capacity planning. Control is the logical connection between work packages, it communicates responsibilities and follows up the progress of work during the project to avoid deviations on the cost, time and quality.

Risk and escalation management is a tool to control hazards and measures to protect the purpose of a project against unwanted effects. This management is used to identify and evaluate risks, and execute actions, action rather than reaction, as soon as possible. This tool is used at regular intervals by the project team, under the project manager of moderation.

Not all the problems, difficulties and additional expenses that arise during a project planning process can be predicted and prevented. Risk and escalation management serves to assist in meeting deadlines and volume requirements, in compliance with the maintenance of project planning costs, investment costs and meeting quality objectives defined in the project proposal (Corrêa, 2010; Corrêa ; Corrêa, 2007; PRADO, 2004a; PRADO, 2004b; CARVALHO; RABECHINI JR, 2008; XAVIER, 2009).

All activities are developed and controlled by a project manager who must be trained in risk and escalation management, and must apply the knowledge continuously in the corresponding projects, along with the full team. There are some defined levels of escalation that depending on the risk classes result in a standardized process. Risks are classified for each project in a list of risks and procedures, and are observed as risk class and measures to follow accordingly in its implementation.

3.3.5 Product Development Process

The process of product development is the guideline for product development projects, and provides the tools for project processing and proactively ensures the product quality. With this process the activities, methods, objectives of the phases and analyzes the decisions with a focus on time, cost and quality are defined. This is a way to guide the project for best practices, transfer knowledge in a uniform way for the company's employees (Slack *et al, 2009;* LIKER; MEIER, 2007; Murman *et al, 2002;* MORGAN; LIKER, 2008).

3.3.6 Teamwork

Teamwork is a form of organization where people work together to perform complex tasks optimally, in order to achieve the company's goals unitedly. In enterprises, teamwork assists for the concentration of each participant on common goals and reinforces the sense of responsibility of all members. It also assists for further development to all employees, and increases the common responsibility. Teamwork helps the company to succeed, it ensures increased identification of employees with the same and increased employee satisfaction, involving everyone in the optimization process (LIKER ; MEIER, 2007;

Murman *et al, 2002*;. LIKER; MEIER, 2008; LIKER; HOSEUS, 2009).

It is greater work efficiency through engaged employees and cooperative with each other. Complex tasks are best mastered and coordinated when using the expertise of individual team members. Therefore one must inform and communicate under standardized ways, the groups should discuss the problems and solutions whenever possible (KEY, 2005; Chaves, 2006).

The organizational climate survey is a tool to assess leadership behavior of a manager, and to develop shared solutions for improving the working environment and collaboration within a given unit. The dialogue between the manager and subordinated employees is moderated by a trained person, with the help of a systematic and standardized process. The climate survey should provide help for self-help. Before or during each shift, employees should dialog with the team in a brief exchange of information. This interchange is needed on the top floor for a better daily work, tasks distribution, objectives achievement, serious errors, current quality situation, new variants, scrap, rework, number of employees (workers on vacation, incapacities). As a suggestion you can have a five-minute dialogue with the team once a day (LIKER; MEIER, 2007; LIKER; MEIER, 2008; LIKER; HOSEUS, 2009; Chaves, 2005; Chaves, 2006).

In the matrix of responsibilities, recurring tasks and activities are clearly documented. These are distributed to responsible groups of people, and each task is defined and, if required, its execution frequency is recorded and documented. Who does what, how and when? Responsibilities on implementing tasks are controlled by visualization. The responsibility matrix is created for all activities and recurring tasks. Documentation is available for each group and displayed publicly. Each employee knows their tasks and follows the designation by the matrix (Santos *et al, 2009*;. Antunes *et al, 2008*;. CORRÊA; Corrêa, 2007; Shingo, 1996; LIKER; MEIER, 2007).

3.3.7 Defect Prevention

Defect prevention means identifying defect sources in the development of products and processes prior to series production, and it also prevents their occurrence by implementing proper measures.

The defect prevention can also be activated by the analysis of shortcomings found, and lessons learned. The later a defect is identified and corrected, the more expensive it gets, since every defect costs time and money. By preventing them in the process to develop products and processes, suppliers should be involved mainly in the development phase. Since the employees know previous difficulties, it is feasible that defects become systematically documented and treated preventively.

There are several tools that can be used to prevent defects; however, we will only be approaching to lean processes and benefits for the whole company.

3.3.8 Standardization

Standardized work explicitly defines the execution of the working process. This must always be performed in the same way, regardless of the person, place or time; each individual pattern represents a particular time, the best and safest way to perform a task, noting that the standardized work becomes transparent through the visual management.

The advantage of standardized work is to uphold standards compliance to ensure sustained efficiency and transparency of working processes, and to make the existing deviations becoming visible. Continuous increases improve security and stability of processes, and promote the employees skills. This method needs the involvement of employees and initiatives to improvement (DAILEY, 2003; LIKER; MEIER, 2007; Murman *et al, 2002;*. CALADO, 2006).

3.3.9 Continuous improvement

The continuous improvement process (CIP) is used for the uninterrupted and consequent enhancement of the whole company, involving all employees in small steps as seen in Figure 06. The improvements achieved are recorded as standard, to ensure its incorporation into the process and eventually transfer to other application areas. As with *kaizen,* what you want is to increase productivity and quality, reduce waste, as well as the rapid implementation of improvement measures, the improvement of workflows and the re-design of jobs. Then, you will be able to achieve shorter *lead times* with staff motivation through not only with the implementation of collective ideas, but with their integration into the company (DAILEY, 2003; MIYAKE, 2008; SLACK *et al, 2009;.* KRAJWSKI *et al, 2009; MARTINS, 2005; JACOBS, 2009; STEVENSON, 2001; MOREIRA, 2008; GAITHER; FRAIZER, 2007; CORRÊA; CORRÊA, 2007;*

SHINGO, 1996; LIKER; MEIER, 2007; MURMANet al., 2002; MORGAN; LIKER, 2008, CAMPOS, 2004, CALADO; LIMA, 2003). The continuous improvement process (CIP) enables a further improvement between the jumps represented by innovations:

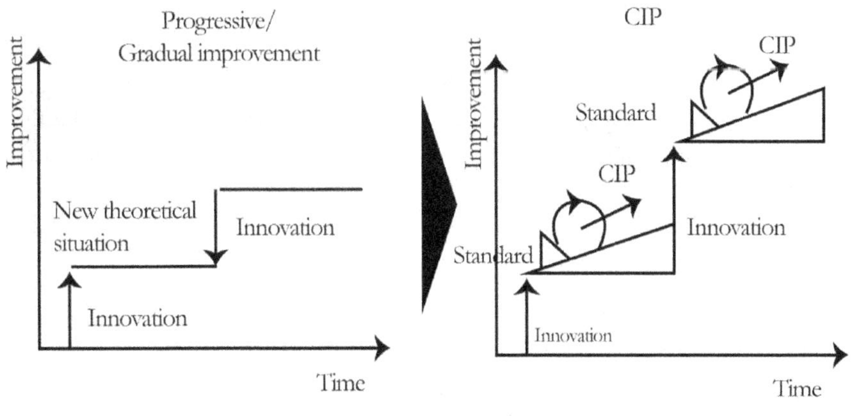

Figure 06: Continuous improvement process (adapted from CAMPOS, 2004).

Troubleshooting techniques are standard systematic procedures used to identify the root causes of problems in order to eliminate them completely. Thus, we do not only analyze the causes of and solutions to problems, but reduce time between identifying and eliminating or correcting problems. The troubleshooting is performed at all levels, with proper tools for each situation (Antunes *et al, 2008;.* STEVENSON, 2001; LIKER; MEIER, 2007; Murman *et al.,* 2002).

Applying the tools for continuous improvement of processes and workflows by scheduling *workshops* for the employees is an alternative for their optimal involvement. It would generate an increasing willingness to strengthen and encourage the employees´ engagement. *Workshops* are run under plans and respond to the need of continuous improvement. These learning experiences allow the participants to present results to managers, facilitate the on-site viewing implementation, and provide the opportunity to monitor results.

3.4 Lean principles and approaches

In engineering and management, it is understood that a manufacturing process is born from a project with functional needs to serve customers, based on designed parameters and a non-rigid structure. In such process, we may identify the five principles of lean thinking organizations and Toyota Production System. According to Womack and Jones (1998), the five principles are considered basic for lean production in the Toyota Production System. They are as follows:

VALUE: capacity offered to a customer at the right time and appropriate price, as defined by the customer.

VALUE CHAIN: specific activities required to design, order and offer a specific product, from concept to release,   from order to delivery, and from raw material to the customer's hands.

FLOW: progressive realization of tasks along the value chain to pass a product from concept to release , from order to delivery, from raw material to the hands of the customer, without the interruption or retro scrap flows.

PULL PRODUCTION: production system with delivery instructions from downstream to upstream activities, in which nothing is produced by the upstream supplier without the downstream customer to signal a need.

PERFECTION: total elimination of any activity that consumes resources but creates no value for all activities over time of a value chain to create value.

In recent decades, the top executives of companies have adopted improvement programs in an effort to transform the companies to successfully compete in the future. As an example of improvement initiatives we have: total quality management, production and distribution systems *(just-in-time),* competition based on time, lean production / lean enterprise, creation of organizations focused on the client, cost management based on activities, *empowerment* of employees and reengineering.

Improvements require major changes, and the goals of these programs are not an increasing or survival improvement, but a performance that enables success in the age of information and knowledge (Kaplan and Norton, 1997).

In order to achieve an excellent manufacture, the principles and the meaningful goals can be implemented. According to the approach of lean production, the methods and tools are derived from principles to achieve the goals. These methods describe the processes -represented by the tools- to be implemented to reach the objectives.

The capabilities over manufacturing processes are widely synchronized and aligned with the methods and tools. According to the approach of Slack *et al.* (2008), Figure 07 describes the objective (lean timing), the approach to overcome the barriers in the implementation of lean synchronization, the methods to eliminate losses , and the various and possible techniques.

In accordance with Feld (2000) and Satolo *et al.* (2000), the methods and techniques generally used in the implementation of lean production, aiming to fight against sources of waste and process improvements, can be grouped into five major groups:

Production Flow - cover methods and techniques related to physical exchanges, product development procedures and definition of necessary standards.

Organization and culture - refers to issues related to the individual, learning, communication and shared values within the organization.

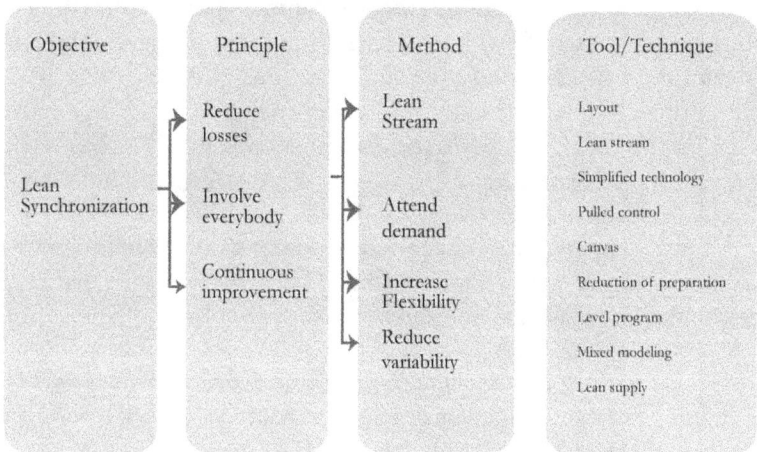

Objective	Principle	Method	Tool/Technique
	Reduce losses	Lean Stream	Layout
			Lean stream
Lean Synchronization	Involve everybody	Attend demand	Simplified technology
			Pulled control
			Canvas
	Continuous improvement	Increase Flexibility	Reduction of preparation
			Level program
		Reduce variability	Mixed modeling
			Lean supply

Figure 07: Lean synchronization (adapted from Slack *et al.*, 2008)

Process Control - addressing methods and techniques related to monitoring, controlling, stabilizing and improving the production process.

Metrics - methods and techniques to measure the performance improvement goals. It rewards the performance of teamwork and employees of the organization.

Logistics — rules and procedures, techniques and methods of planning and control of internal and external material flows of the organization.

In any case, the greatest goal of the lean method is to reduce waste so that the company's results can be increased.

CHAPTER 04
LEAN STARTUP

We have discussed in the previous chapters what a startup is. But it is important to think where this term came from. Well, the word *startup* comes from *start*, which means:

Start
start

n 1 Departure, beginning (of a movement, travel, race etc.). **2** beginning, kick-off, outset. **3** pull, push, momentum. **4** start, scare. **5** advantage, front. **6** starting place. **7** starter (motor). **8** release, assign. **9** cause, give. **10** establish (business). (Michaellis Dictionary).

To establish a successful business, the lean startup methodology needs to be developed. It is an approach that seeks to eliminate the waste of time and resources spent on the effort of trying to understand what customers really want. The task of the *Lean Startup* is to find "a synthesis between the company's vision and what customers accept: not surrender to what customers think they want or tell clients what they should want" (RIES, 2012).

On the Lean Startup studies by Eric Ries, Hart (2012), he states that the "use of the term *Lean* is consistent with the management philosophy of the Toyota Production System. In this context, it is an approach that tries to minimize the use of spending anything other than creates value for the customer. "

As we saw in Chapter 03, the lean method prioritizes relations with customers from the initial formation of the product to the making in the production line.

The Lean Startup proposal meets the first two principles of Lean Product Development cited by Morgan and Liker (2008). These are "to identify the value set by the client to separate value of waste and focus efforts early in the product development process to fully explore alternative solutions while there is a maximum design flexibility."

Thus, Ries, 2012 (pages 7 and 8) points out the five principles of *Lean Startup*:

1st Entrepreneurs are everywhere;

2nd Undertaking is to manage;

3rd Validated learning;

4th Build-measure-learn;

5th Accounting for innovation.

We better understand each of these principles:

Entrepreneurs are everywhere:

In the early chapters we briefly discussed about entrepreneurship issues and on the startups stages in the country. Today people effectively seek to venture more, either by opportunity or by necessity. Even universities are giving more emphasis to entrepreneurship, and the dimension of its demand.

But, forgetting all this and looking at the world around us, we always find someone undertaking projects: it can be someone selling water at a red light or in a luxurious supermarket. There is always an entrepreneur around us.

To undertake is to manage:

This statement should not surprise anyone. To undertake is to manage: cash, production, people, team, ideas. It is to manage results and achieve goals. There are successful entrepreneurs who do not have a successful business.

It may not be the entrepreneur (partner) that manages the entire company, but it sure was he/she who set up the team and knew how to manage people; for it to be where now he/ she is.

Validated learning:

Startups are to learn how to develop a sustainable business, and so forth to validate it scientifically.

Build - measure - learn:

The tripod turning ideas into products, measuring customer's reactions and learning from them will be referred later on.

It is essential to understand the lean startup method , is as well as to sum up the step-by-step process to turn ideas into profitable businesses.

Figure 08 briefly demonstrates how this cycle works:

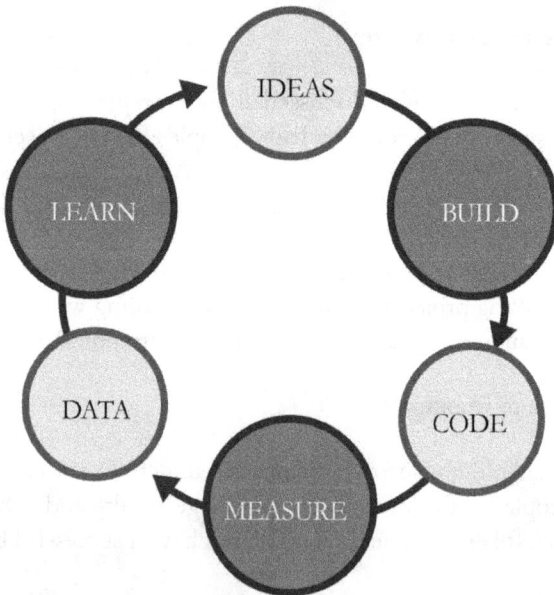

Figure 08: Build - measure - learn cycle. Ries, 2010.

Accounting for innovation:

Measuring progress, setting milestones and prioritizing work is accounting for innovation. Instead of blaming people for something that didn't go as planned is necessary to understand "why" it didn't go as planned, what actually went wrong, what people had to do, why they didn't, what they were missing, method, standard. It might also be possible that customers do not want to buy the product as it is presented as they expect a change and modification.

This important information has to be gotten from the customers, so it assures the company's growth. After all, the target audience feedback will tell us what the best path to take is.

4.1 From conceiving ideas to capturing them in paper.

As previously mentioned, one of the five principles of *Lean Startup that catch*es our attention is the tripod "build, measure and learn - turn ideas into products, creating something for customers, measure your results with customers, learn from *feedback* customers and rebuild from what you learned."

This tripod is very similar to the PDCA cycle (Plan, Do, Check and Action), which is a known method and used to maintain, improve, and innovate products, services and processes. It also makes them converge in two ways: first, the realization of successive changes in operational or administrative proceedings with successive gains without investment, continuous improvement, and growth of activities to create more value with less action in reducing the consumption of resources. This is known in business as continuous improvement or Kaizen. The second form of convergence of PDCA is the act of designing a new process to achieve the desired goal or making substantial changes to existing processes. This is called Kaikaku, where major advances lead to radical improvement and new investments (Calado, 2010).

The chart shown below represents the correlation of the PDCA cycle with the *Lean Startup methodology.*

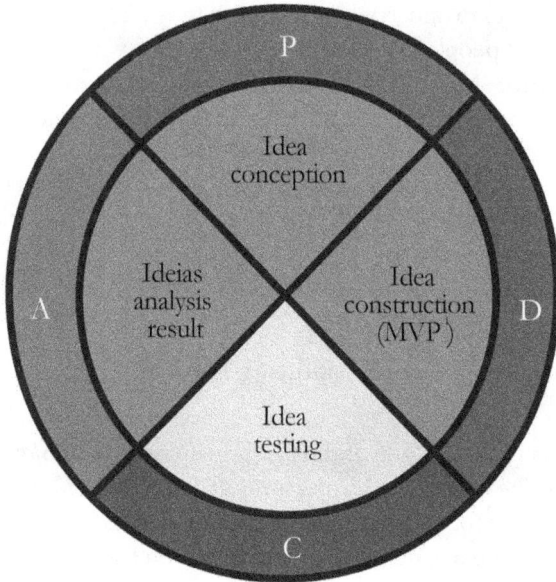

Figure 09: Contraposition of the PDCA cycle with the Lean Startup methodology

(¹ MVP - Minimum Viable Product - product prototype that aims to understand what product expectations the customer has).

Despite the development of new products and services, it is encouraging and challenging to make it happen. Thus, one cannot expect to have the design finished for new products or services, it is actually necessary to test various ideas and concepts until they set the general concept to pursue what we want (Slack, 2009).

The *Lean Startup* approach relates exactly to this development stage of a product, as we can see in the following figure:

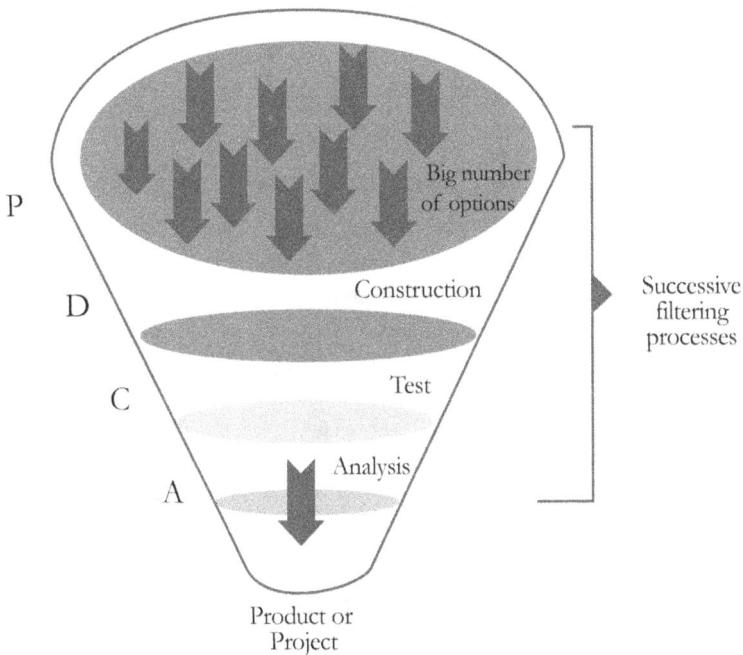

Figure 10: Use of the Lean Startup methodology in successive processes of ideas filtration in the design of new products or services (based on Slack, 2009).

A modern company should be customer oriented, so forth planning with the customer is important. It is for you to have it on top of your business model, with the purpose of generating competitive advantage, as stated by Kotler and Keller, 2006. In order to effectively be advantageous, it is essential to understand what the customer searches in your product or service.

Knowing your customer this way would be extremely important for all companies. However, for a startup it can be a "life or death" matter. One that doesn't know his client well can invest absolutely everything in a product or service, even if it might not sell, and consequently would cause its closure.

Seeking to minimize this possibility, Ries 2012 insists that all *startup* procedures should always work within the loop *build, measure and learn*, allowing learning the most important part of the process. Consequently, it allows the entrepreneur to rebuild the project / product more assertively and as expected by the customer.

In the development of a successful enterprise, making errors is inevitably expected. The creation of management accordingly, and the continuous innovation of a company should be based on developing a simple initial product and sell it to initial customers, taking into consideration their feedback which will help you develop the ideal product (RIES, 2012).

Anyone who believes these "errors" increase the waste is being a fool. In fact, when a low risk company is launched, having the product tested directly in the market segment and with customers feedback, they will always help to make the necessary adjustments in the product. Being helped by the organization and the discovery of faster opportunities, the most important thing is that the product development becomes agile and according to the customers´ need (BLANK and RIES, 2012).

The lean startup method is used in the product on the market, therefore this methodology alone will not save the life of the company, but it will definitely assist over the integration process of your product in the market. That is, when the product is positioned in the market, it will go through all its natural life cycle, and use other strategies and methods needed to reach its maturity. According to Kotler (2012) when the product reaches its maturity, it needs to be revised and updated to avoid its decline. RIES (2012) states that at this time the company can see this "new product" as a new startup and use it up for lean startup again. Figure 03 represents the products life cycle moment when a start-up can make use of this methodology.

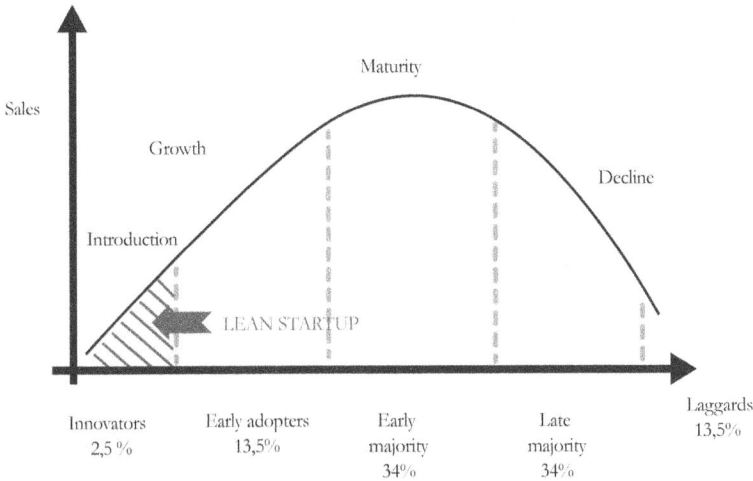

Figure 11: Product life cycle: product phase in which we use the Lean Startup methodology

To use the *Lean Startup* methodology entrepreneurs need to first know what the goal is, "where he plans to get". Consequently, to identify the current need of the customer would be required by testing the market with minimum viable products **that** must be manufactured in compliance *of the lean methodology,* i.e. waste reduction. This verification can be done by comparing two minimum viable products when the test is all judgmental assumptions, when the customer tells his experience with the product, or even testing every improvement made.

To analyze the results is necessary to make use of the scientific and statistical tools, and guarantee reliability. Thereby the test will show if the company is on course for success, whether you walk towards the established goals or failure; if it is contrary to what is aimed.

When the results are positive, the entrepreneur must consider what its growth engine will be, what aspects will make the business grow sustainable, noting that all products and services have a life cycle and therefore innovation processes must be continuous.

When results are negative, that the product is pivoted becomes essential, i.e. restart it or give it up. This is not an easy decision; therefore it should be taken along with the company staff, employees, managers, sponsors and investors.

4.2 Minimum Viable Product – MVP

The MVP is not a prototype, a reduced version of your product: it is the first product to be marketed.

As Ries states (2012, page 85), "MVP helps entrepreneurs start the learning process as quickly as possible. However, it is not necessarily the lowest conceivable product; it is, alone, the fastest way to go through the cycle build-measure-learn feedback with the least possible effort. "

To develop the MVP, entrepreneurs need to consider:

Target audience (Client)

Core values of this public

Features the entrepreneur has at hand (money, raw materials, etc.)

Development of the resources with the product that meet the corresponding values

The MVP is not the finished product: it is a product to be sold, tested and validated by the market. Thus, the entrepreneur cannot use all his chances at once in this MVP.

To validate the MVP, entrepreneurs need to put it on the market and test it directly with the target audience.

4.3 Business Models

The business model helps the entrepreneur to take his role earnestly, and it also provides answers to the four questions stated by the MVP.

According to Alexander Osterwalder (2010), a business model describes creative logic, delivery and captures value by an organization. It shows how the company will become sustainable, and profitable. And most importantly, the forms the company will use to give value to their customers.

Among all existing business models, the one that has been mostly used by startups is "Canvas, the Business Model" by Alexander Osterwalder. It is a visually attractive model, it gives the business a systemic view, it is conceived altogether as a team and partners, it is simple to do and easy to apply, giving agility and speed in decision making, the one entrepreneurs need when venturing in their business.

It is not to avoid using the Strategic Plan of the company's business (the one with executive summary, mission, vision, principles and values, strategic marketing, financial, production and HR plan). On the contrary, we are prompting you to start your business with the Business Model, and get the market feedback to design the Strategic Business Plan. However, instead of drawing up the *plan* only with empirical data and research, you will have real market data, collected from the sale of its minimum viable product.

Thus, startups are the ones to implement a Business Model. This is to be the first step. Let us keep in mind that a startup is any endeavor that involves uncertainty; it can be anything from a new product within an existing organization to a new company.

A well-designed business model is created jointly with partners or team members, all involved in the project in question. This is the only way to ensure a consistent and appropriately lined model to the project objectives.

The Canvas Business Model is divided into 9 quadrants: customers, value proposition, channels, relationship, source of revenue, key activities, key features, key partners and main costs. Let us look at each of these items:

Clients: Who will you attend? What is the suggested solution? And last, who will pay the bill?

Value proposition: what do you (your company, business) offer to this client? Nowadays people have access to so many products and services, so consider the following questions : why will your customer buy from you and not your competitor? What will you "sell" or "offer" differently? If we turn to the former Strategic Business Plan, you will come up with the only answer: your business strategy. For example, if I ask what Kopenhagem sells, the fastest answer will be *chocolate!* But this business is short-sighted by meaning the product itself! In fact what Kopenhagem sells are *gifts.* This is the business strategy, and it is the reason why it can charge a lot more for 100g of chocolate than Nestlé, for example. Another argument: if you buy a 160gram Nestlé chocolate bar and give it to your boyfriend or girlfriend, perhaps you get some frustrating or disappointing reactions; but if you take two 20gr truffles from Kopenhagem, the guy will be much happier. Therefore, what will your gift be?

Channels: how will you deliver these values to your customers? How will your client come to you? How will you sell your product or service?

 Relationship: the way to interact and sustain the client. This is what is famously called post-sale. It is the strategy you will use to ensure your client being loyal to you.

Key activities: everything you need to make your project happen; thus, you have to keep in mind that if you fail in the procedures, nothing will happen.

Key features: resources you need to enable key activities. These are the essential items not to be missed when developing your business.

Key partners: the potential people or companies have to help you. Remember, we cannot fulfill anything if we are alone.

Costs: the main costs to conduct your business. They are usually linked to key resources and key activities.

Following is the example of the Business Model Canvas of Sýndreams:

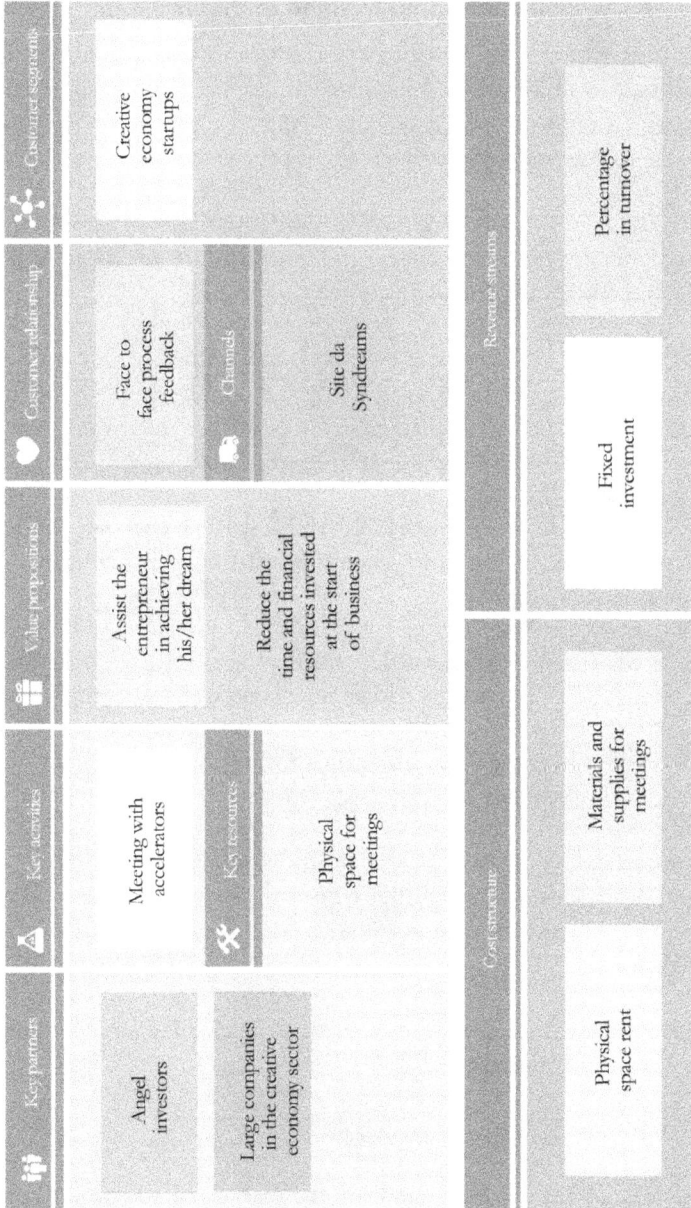

Key partners	Key activities	Value propositions	Customer relationship	Customer segments
Angel investors	Meeting with accelerators	Assist the entrepreneur in achieving his/her dream	Face to face process feedback	Creative economy startups
Large companies in the creative economy sector	Key resources: Physical space for meetings	Reduce the time and financial resources invested at the start of business	Channels: Site da Sýndreams	

Cost structure		Revenue streams	
Physical space rent	Materials and supplies for meetings	Fixed investment	Percentage in turnover

4.4 How is the Lean Startup understood in Brazil?

It is difficult to present how Brazilian entrepreneurs understand the Lean Startup, since it is still newly used in our country. Very recently, when there were some to venture, we had two ways of proceeding:

1st Do: without studying the market, without knowledge, without validation. Those with money rented a property and started. If it worked - great; if it went wrong - everything was lost.

2nd Think and then do: a business plan was drawn up (the one presented by scholars and administrators long ago). By the time it was ready, we initiated the project, but as a rule, the plan went into a drawer and it was never used.

So long in Brazil, that is the way the entrepreneurial culture advanced until then. And culture is something rooted, unlikely to be changed. Today, even having novel forms to venture, our entrepreneurs keep repeating what we previously envisioned:

-Some entrepreneurs believe that getting "lean startup" is just having a good idea, a business model and an angel investor;

-Others consider they need to validate their hypothesis, and test their prototype in the laboratory to see if it works;

There are some who work on the business model, design the validation strategies of the idea, and when they come to "do" (validate the market), they forget everything already planned and do everything the way they "think" it will work.

To realize that two elements are needed is the essential component before making major investments:

a)To have a good business model;

b)To validate this business model in the market, i.e. to develop customers for the created product.

Now then, the biggest difference perceived between Americans and Brazilians, is the ease of those first mentioned to have their endeavors follow a pivot process.

Since there has been created an "all or nothing"- culture, Brazilians do not have the same facility. That is, if the entrepreneur did not achieve good results the first time he becomes a "man of failure" to society.

The mentality of "we can't make mistakes, you must always be right" was promoted, and had the businessman to face difficulties to pivot when required.

I recently met an entrepreneur who dealt with exactly this problem: the product was very good, but he was selling it to the wrong audience without noticing. Despite the fact that the product was not being sold, he continued to insist on it until the situation became despairing. Eventually he went broke.

Nowadays, looking back to what he did, we can reflect the product was not to be sold on a large scale. It was a high added value to be sold to a very specific audience. That is, the investment could have been much lower and in much higher return, so he had to have paid more attention to market signals and pivoted the business. In this case, he would have closed the factory with more than 500m² and outsourced production.

But again, for him that would mean he did not succeed with his venture; it would also be unconceivable to say that all began with more than 500m² factory, and it was now in a little room over 50m² .

Anyway, this difficulty hasn't been experienced in American or other Anglo-Saxon cultures. It has been much more common in Latin populations.

WARNING: These characteristics are not a rule. They are just noticeable features over years of mentoring and consulting with companies and entrepreneurs. Like everything, there are exceptions.

A profitable business is not successful only through methods and business models. It is also necessary to implement some administrative tools to assure the goal is reached. Remember to undertake is to manage.

But after all, what is a tool?

Tool
to.ol

sf (en tool) **1** Any instrument or utensil used in the arts or crafts.**2** A set of utensils.**3** Fragment of sugarcane used in pottery to decorate the dish parts.Reg **4** (Ceará) Cowboy Spurs. (Michaellis Dictionary).

Finally, the tools are to assist in difficult jobs, making them easier. Managing a business has never been easy, and even today is certainly much more difficult.

In the past our principal competitor was our neighbor; our less enlightened ideas were great innovations. Today, when we think of something new we must first search to see if it is really new. Our competitors are anywhere in the world, and often more competitive than we are.

Our customers are looking for innovation, convenience, delivery time, quality, among many other things. And to win this battle we need to be very competitive. But what to do, how to become competitive when starting a business?

Let us not reinvent the wheel, instead I suggest we look at the administrative tools that already exist and can be of help.

5.1 Environment Analysis

Before you come up with your idea, you probably made an environment analysis, which may have been informally done. You just had an idea after realizing that someone needs something and nobody offers, or who does, hasn't offer quality; whether it is in the closest place or 100km away.

Furthermore, you saw an opportunity in the market that can be anything. But to realize this opportunity, you were paying attention to your surroundings.

In academic literature we separate environment as: internal, micro and macro environment. That simple! Look at Figure 12.

In the *internal environment* we have the company and all its sectors. In the *micro environment* we have the stakeholders that relate more closely with the company, and in the *macro environment* we have the market in general, with its political, economic and social changes.

When we think of our business, we need to analyze each of these variables; by doing it, we can understand whether or not it is right time to initiate a startup. This analysis helps us to reduce the risks.

But let us consider,   it is not made only on the first day of the project and go. It needs to be seen and revised frequently, as things change, and very fast.

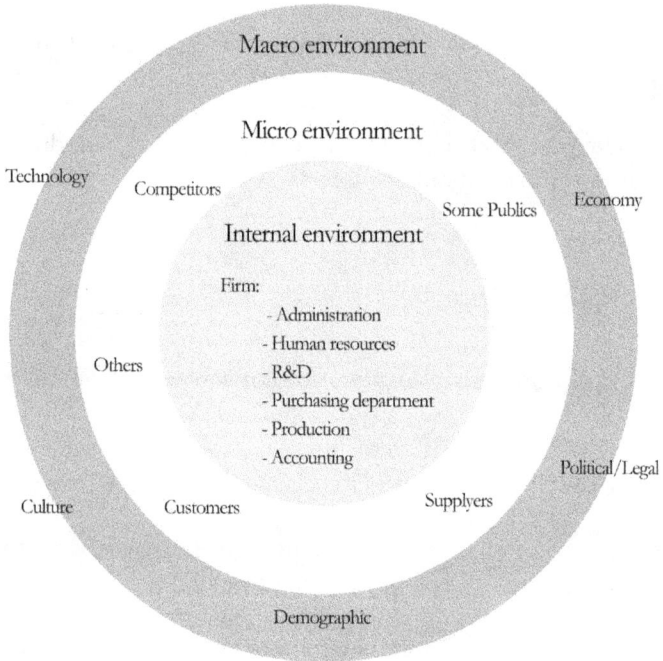

Figure 12: Graphical representation of the Environment Analysis

5.2 SWOT Analysis

Notice on the following:

-SWOT: Strength, Weakness, Opportunity, and Threat.

Let us clarify that SWOT analysis is a summary table of the company's environmental analysis. This is to say that all we examined earlier, it can be organized in the following framework quadrants:

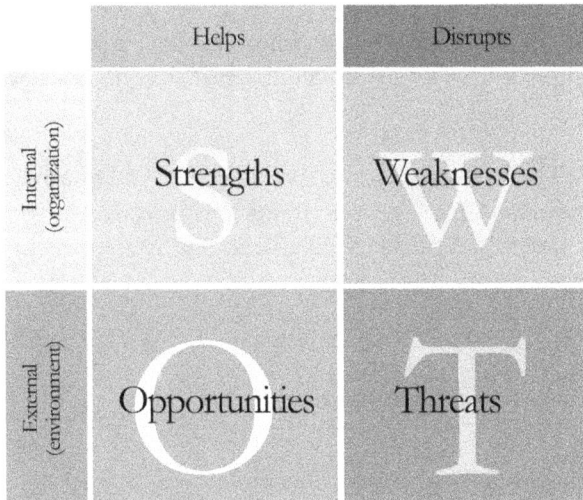

	Helps	Disrupts
Internal (organization)	Strengths	Weaknesses
External (environment)	Opportunities	Threats

Figure 13: Graphical representation of SWOT Analysis

-Strength is all that helps your business grow, all good and positive elements;

-Weakness is all bad things or failures your company has;

-Opportunities are the gaps you saw in the macro or micro environment, and the ones you can attend.

-Threats are also in the macro and micro environment, and may hinder you from getting your goals achieve.

We have to consider and say competitors are not a threat, not here, not even in China. If you notice your competitor can "spoil" your business is because you have some weaknesses your competitors don't. Therefore, find out what your weaknesses are and correct them. If you fail don't "blame" them. For example: my competitor sells cheaper than my company. Great, he is more efficient and effective in production, can negotiate a better price with suppliers and thus has a lower cost. In this case, your weaknesses are: low efficiency and effectiveness, difficulty when negotiating prices with suppliers, high operating cost. I know it's easier to blame someone, but it will not solve your problems.

After the SWOT matrix is ready, observe the results and research about What is true in your action market, opportunities or threats? Do you have more strengths or weaknesses? Balance all aspects and make a decision, whether you continue or not with the project.

5.3 Budget Sheets and Cash Flow

Here are two other important tools for monitoring the development of the enterprise: budget and cash flow. One helps entrepreneur to have a plan to follow in the outputs and inputs of cash, how much you need to sell effectively, where you can spend and what you should do with the money (budget). The other shows whether the budget projections were carried out or not; if it didn't, it would give the scale data of what could have happened, and it would tell you where the fault of money is (cash flow).

Budget: the set of plans and policies that formally established and expressed financial results, it allows the administration to know a priori the operating results of the company, and then run the necessary trimmings to be achieved and the possible deviations to be analyzed, evaluated and corrected (MOREIRA, p. 15, 1989).

Cash Flow: the source of all the money that came in as cash, and the application of all the money that came out as cash in a given period, offering as a result the financial flow of the company (IUDÍCIBUS and MARION, p 123, 2000).

It is to be clear that none of the two tools whether there are profits or losses in the company, as this is the function of Income Statement of any period, prepared by accountants based on the company's day (cash flow).

To a better understanding, a company with cash on hand is not always a company with profits, nor is even a company out of cash one with losses. I know it sounds complicated, but it is not.

For example, a company may be out of cash due to an uncapitalization due to a large purchase of raw materials. However, this material becomes a product to be sold, billed and the customer will pay when received. When today the company is out of cash, tomorrow it will have a profit (what follows to production is selling).

Soon after, the same company delivers the goods and receives the payments from the client, and since there might not have other orders at the moment, there will be no need to buy more raw material, taking received value to cash income. Hence, it has a positive result in the cash flow.

But if it does not get any more orders, the company will not sell. And without sales there is no profit, despite having cash on hand.

Anyway, SEBRAE, ENDEAVOR and other professional associations constantly offer courses and training on Financial Management. So forth, knowing and going deeper on the subject is worthwhile.

5.4 Some other tools

In management there are numerous other tools to help the entrepreneur to become better managers in their business. Even though, the goal of this book is to apply the lean startup in startup companies, we will not stick to those that we are sure you will use after validating your idea in the market.

Still, we show a short list of tools that you must learn to use to continue standing out in the market:

-Value Flow Mapping

-Just in Time and Kanban

-Kaisen

-Visual Management

-Continuous Improvement Programs - Jidoka

-Standardized work

Find
fi.nd

(lat Incontrare) vtd and vpr **1** Hatch against; hit. vpr **2** stumbling. Vtd **3** Compensate a sum or installment credit with debt. Vpr **4** Dispute, fight, oppose. Vpr **5** Hitting a duel. Vtd Finding **6;** across, run into. vtd **7** Discover.**8** Give the guy with.**9** Give the front; bump.10. Get 11. Being, to find himself in.12. Joining at the same point.**13** having casual or Due conference.

In the previous chapters we briefly discussed about the entrepreneurial scene, about the tools that entrepreneurs currently have to make use of, and the innovative nature a business like a Startup must have.

But how do we joint all that and turn it into something tangible? How will an entrepreneur in the current scenario create a successful startup using the administrative tools? We will clear it up.

6.1 Proposed method to accelerate entrepreneurship actions

To speed up entrepreneurship activities I suggest the use of the Lean Startup methodology, which I will go into deeper detail in the following pages.

To begin the process, the first analysis is whether the business is effectively a startup or not, if there is innovation, a real discussion about what the market is, who the customers are, what their needs and desires are, the values they seek, who will pay the service or product, and what these customers are willing to pay. The answers you come up with will help you in designing the MVP.

The idea is to define the sale strategy for MVP and estimate a minimum return on investment so far. Get your hands dirty. Go out into the market to test and validate the product or service (along with guidelines and the tests that have been presented in the previous chapter).

In the end, the entrepreneur knows whether it is worth or not to continue with the project. If he is able to climb your business or not; if you will need an angel investor, whether or not he can touch the startup only with the offered resources.

To lighten on this journey, we will present the whole process in three steps.

6.2 Process Steps

We specify this acceleration process in three steps, which rely on the SWOT tool. They are as follows:

Step 1: Entrepreneurship activity definition (30 days)

PLAN: Analysis of market environment to undertake the project;

PLAN: Business Model Construction;

PLAN: MVP Definition (Minimum Viable Product).

Step 2: Setting Strategies (30 days)

PLAN: Defining goals and strategies;

PLAN: Financial Advice;

DO: Presentation of MVP ready for operation.

Step 3: Up> Monitoring and Adjustments (120 days)

DO: Company Sales and activities

CHECKING: Monitoring of the activities held for four months.

ACTION: Adjustments needed to achieve the goal.

Step 4: Evaluation (1 day)

CHECKING: program evaluation and feedback.

The full implementation of this method is given in 6 months, maximum period for which the entrepreneur puts his idea on the market and tests it. One could ask about six months being the maximum period. We all have ideas, needs, and opportunities. If we delay too much in taking our idea from paper to action, for sure someone else will do it and then the project would cease from being a pioneer, and become just a copy of someone who is already doing it.

6.3 Liability and responsibilities of entrepreneurs

Entrepreneurs are responsible for their business ventures. Thus, they need to study the market, understand the customer, meet the needs of the target audience, and know the resource limits.

In addition, the entrepreneur is one who gets their hands dirty and turns strategy into action. It is he who receives feedback from the market and needs to analyze what is effective and just right for the customer.

The methods and tools are to help. Mentors and the accelerators reveal them the paths. But the entrepreneur is the one who needs to follow it.

To further clarify these steps, we will present each separately in the following chapters.

Define
de.fi.ne

(Definire lat) vtd   **1** Give a definition: It is possible to define evil?
Defined in a few words that idea. "The author wanted to define
them for contrast" (Rui Barbosa).   vtd   **2** Determine, fix. Vtd   **3**
demarcate, fix: It is recommended that each define its position
vtd.   **4** Interpret: I do not see how to set this tribute vtd **5** Give the
distinctive qualities of:.. His first words were enough to set it vpr   **6**
Take a resolution or party:. In this regard we have defined in vtd   **7**
Making known. Vtd   **8** Expose accurately. Vtd   **9** Exposing the
many faces or sides.

The definition of the process is the beginning of this journey: what the
business is, for whom it is so important, what needs will be met with the
product or service.

This stage is divided into 3 parts: the market environment analysis for the enterprise, the construction of the business model, and the definition of the minimum viable product.

7.1 Market environment analysis for the entrepreneurial project

Here the entrepreneur needs to answer two basic questions related to your business development: what aspects help, and which ones hinder.

It is essential that the answers are all encompassed: from the lack of time to devote to the project (which hinders) to the deep knowledge your partner has on the product to be developed (which helps). Everything, absolutely everything must be noted. If there are doubts among what elements help or which hinder (for example: we do not have commercial room – this would help because we do not pay the rent, though it would harm, because I have no customers to receive), the entrepreneur must write the item in two columns.

To start, write your ideas here.

Help		Hinder	

When this process is finished, we separate the items that help depending on the entrepreneur and the firm to happen (internal variables), and not depending on the entrepreneur or company to happen (external variables). We will do similarly with the items to come.

To start, write your ideas here.

Help		Disrupt	
It depends on the entrepreneur (Internal)	It depends on the market (External)	It depends on the entrepreneur (Internal)	It depends on the market (External)

After this process we have the initial SWOT Analysis for the Startup.

To start, write your ideas here.

	Help	Hinder
Internal	**Strengths**	**Weaknesses**
External	**Opportunities**	**Threats**

I say initial SWOT because we are just starting. There are many changes that can and will happen over the course of this startup and as we previously saw, SWOT is a picture of the moment, the now.

This initial "screenshot" is important because it would measure from the beginning if the business in mind will be possibly developed or not. This is to say that if someone suddenly has the idea of a hardware device that can fit 3.1MB files, it would be great. However, this idea is obsolete, now we have devices with 60GB.

That example is extreme, but it is important to clarify the reason why we have to start with the analysis of the market.

Anyway, after identifying the strengths and weaknesses, threats and opportunities, we reinforce on the most important to focus, which are your strengths and opportunities. Do not worry about the weakening aspects, but concentrate on enforcing what it is offered to your plan.

You might be asking yourself: "but I learned that I should develop strategies to address the weaknesses and threats... why the transposition?" Your business does not exist, it is still on paper. So if you have to deal with the weaknesses and threats, you have to take the opportunity and make it happen before your competitor does.

Please note I did not say to forget your weaknesses and threats, but focus your efforts on the strengths and opportunities. Track and measure the threats and weaknesses regularly, but do not forsake working on opportunities.

There is an exception. If you came to the conclusion that one of the weaknesses or threats prevents you from doing your deal happen, then yes, you need to rethink these tips. However, what is important to point out is that money is not a reason to stop thinking in your business. The development of the minimum viable product will be studied next.

7.2 Building the Business Model

Building the business model is designed after the entrepreneur thinks and reviews the SWOT, and adds the collected information taken from the market.

I suggest using the Business Model Canvas, which as previously seen, it effectively summarizes the first steps of the project.

At this point, the entrepreneur needs to answer some important questions related to the product and the clients:

- Who is your customer? Who is the target audience?

 -What are the values customers search in a product or similar service delivered by the Startup? What elements will you draw in the customer to call his attention and buy from you?

- How will you deliver these values to your customers? Which channel would you use to do it?

- How do you intend to relate to your customer? How do you ensure the customer coming back to buy from you? How will he be loyal to you?

- Who pays for the values offered? Is it the client? Will the customer pay monthly or by product?

Right after, the entrepreneur answers some important points about the progress of activities within the startup:

- What are the main activities your Startup needs to ensure the value delivery to customers? It is important you list the activities. So, what is not in the list is not a priority.

- What are the key resources for these activities to happen? Only the resources connected with the above mentioned activities should appear.

- Who are your partners in this endeavor? Who are the companies, people, and entities that can help you to perform the key activities and bring the product to your customer? It should be partners, not suppliers. If the carrier will charge you as it does with everyone, it is not your partner, but your provider.

To start, write your ideas here.

And finally, what are main costs you have associated with key resources? It is important to mention as an example that if you have an e-commerce, and your customers are not going to you, there is no personal contact. Consequently, the key resources would not consider physical business location to meet customers. customers. Therefore within the main costs will not appear as "rent of your local"; it is not a cost attached to key resources or the development of your business.

After giving an answer to these questions, we have the Business Model Canvas of the startup ready. That is, the conception of the idea, the first quadrant of the Lean Startup method is closed. But this is the first model, it must be tested and validated, and for it we use the minimum viable product, our next topic.

7.3 Definition of the minimum viable product

Here is the most important step in the acceleration process. Now is the time for the entrepreneur to set his first product, the one he will put on the market and actually the one to be sold.

It is essential to emphasize that an MVP is not a poor or a cheaper version of the final product. It is actually the product that addresses key values under CANVAS developed previously.

Let us elaborate this idea: in a furniture designer business model, the entrepreneur identified that his client's main value was the material quality, usability and personalization in the product; the designed and created furniture must count with these features to attract customers; i.e. it does not make sense just to create a piece of furniture full of details that in the end would not be useful but decorative. It has to be useful tool in everyday life. In this example, as one of the values is the customization, the entrepreneur can create drawings and sketches, and "sell" these items initially without the obligation to build. If he/she wants a specific product, it can be created in demand considering personalization.

We could have another example in software creation. Before investing thousands of dollars, the entrepreneur can validate his/her idea testing it on a worksheet with macros and functions.

For example, if the entrepreneurs can deploy to a real company and state that this "program" is better and can help them in every needs, they can move forward with their project and invest a higher value in the development of the software itself but if he/she has answers like: does the same as the other, did not change anything, it's the same thing ... he or she would need to review his or her initial idea, and possibly pivot his or her business.

The fact above is real, the entrepreneur had the idea of developing a specific software to control from the input of raw materials through production, monitoring the residue and processing it into another product (seeking to meet one of the articles in the new local legislation called " Solid Waste Law "). As much as the idea seemed great, the response obtained from customer was: "I will not need it for the next two years ... we have no interest in this product today, but come back with it when the law will truly generate a fine to us!!!" . Now as a result, the entrepreneur pivoted his initial idea and now he gives consulting work and advice for companies in the environmental sector, helping them on the needs and waste storing procedures. That is, he discovered a real customer need to this day. This strategy was not applied two years ago.

If he had invested what intended with the purpose of having the software, he would have lost the money used to specialize in the subject of 'Environment' , and ended up having effective return.

Thus, the MVP is not only the simplest version of the product, it meets the values of customers and nothing else. All the "plus", the "pomp", the "extra" will be placed later in the next versions, by necessity and effective market desire.

In some cases, there is not an alpha and a beta version of the product, as in the case of already patented products. When this happens, we work with an

"MVP" for sales channels. In this example, we chose one of the channels displayed on the Canvas and invested our efforts on it. We measured the results and checked the return.

This actually happened with an entrepreneur. She sold "chic" (fancy) bags for pregnant women. These bags with maternity fashion concept from the outside looked like a handbag from a designer, but in the inside, it had all the slots and other benefits of the common maternity bag.

There is no possibility that an MVP existed for the bag, since it is a fashion bag and therefore it needs to follow the trends, but the sale channel can be chosen as a MVP: multibrand shops, owned stores, e-commerce, etc.

In this specific case, she started with the e-commerce and what she found was amazing: the bag generated interest in mothers. Of course, most of the customers were women who had their day started very early and finished late at night; therefore, they had to often carry a change of clothes, umbrella, bottle of water, tea, cereal bars, and other women things. In the inside the bag was waterproof and kept the food warm for a certain period of time (characteristic of maternity bags).

These are points for the entrepreneur, who initially planned to sell her handbags for pregnant women in multi-brand shops. Because of her choice of selling in e-commerce, she discovered her true target audience: women in general, not just pregnant. This expanded the initial vision of the market and the time to invest in other products, now to the right audience.

To carry out the construction of the MVP, we finished the second quadrant of the Lean Startup method. Now we must define the product sale strategies, and figure out the points of attention and analysis to close our two remaining quadrants: to test the idea and study the results.

To start, write your ideas here .

WHAT ARE THE MAIN VALUES YOUR CUSTOMERS SEEK ?

TRY TO TURN EACH OF THESE VALUES INTO "SOMETHING TANGIBLE"

88

JOIN THE PALPABLE PARTIES: WHAT'S YOUR MVP?

Strategy
s.tra.te.gy

sf (gr strategia) **1** Art to conceive warfare operation with joints plans.
2 Catch, craftiness, artifice.**3** Art of driving complex things. Var:
strategic.

It is now time to go to the battlefront. However, you need to know what to
do there, what the goal is and how to win the war. There might be too many
questions, but only one answer: plan strategies. This is what we will do in this
second stage. This does not mean the minimum viable product is ready; the
entrepreneur often needs more time to finish it, and it is OK. Now it is time
to split time and perform tasks simultaneously.

To start this phase, the entrepreneur needs to know what the total cost of his/
her minimum viable product is.

We emphasize that the continual nature of the process, and the definition
of strategies and goals often assist the entrepreneur in the completion of his
product.

8.1 Definition of goals and strategies

This is an important step and we need to start with the following question:
how does the entrepreneur intend to get a return, in real numbers, with MVP
sales? Remember that to reach the needed and possible number is at the same
time challenging.

Once you know this number, we formulate the other questions: what is the cost of your product? What price is the market willing to pay? How do your direct or indirect competitors sell?

To start, write your ideas here.

Answer the questions:

How much do you pretend to have in return in 4 months?

Answer:

How much your product cost?

Answer:

How much is the market willing to pay?

Answer:

How much competitors charge for their products?

Answer:

Then we do the simple initial calculation: sale price minus the total cost. Afterward, we divide the value entrepreneurs want to have in returns by the "unit profit", and in consequence we will have the amount of products we need to sell within the stipulated period.

Example:

The product cost: R $ 120.00

Average selling price in the market: R $ 400.00

"Unit Profit": R $ 280.00

Entrepreneur Goal: R $ 28,000.00 at the end of the acceleration process (4 months test on the market)

Account:

R $ 28,000 / US $ 280 = 100 products

IMPORTANT: we use simple initial calculation because the total cost is not yet identified, i.e. the following is not yet taken into account: electricity cost, Internet, telephone, other costs to sell the product, etc. This is actually the initial targets discussion that can be reviewed in the future.

To start, write your ideas here.

Make your calculations:

Product Cost: R $ _____

Average selling price in the market: R $ _____

"Unit Profit": R $ _____

Entrepreneur Goal: R $ _____ at the end of the acceleration process (4 months test on the market)

Account:

$$\frac{\text{_____}}{\text{Meta Entrepreuneur / Income Unit}} \quad = \quad \frac{\text{_____}}{\substack{\text{Qtd Products} \\ \text{to sell}}}$$

After the definition of 100 products sold in four months -> goal, we ask then how the entrepreneur intends to divide this sale. He believes he will be able to sell 25 units in each month, or he will sell less in the first month since no one knows yet. However, it is believed that with the mouth-through-mouth method he will sell more in the 4th month. This largely depends on the entrepreneur's profile, the chosen product and the target audience. There is no right or wrong answer, it all depends on the assessment made in the SWOT the first meeting.

Following this definition, the entrepreneur 'designs' the sales strategy, and customer and partner approach. A step-by-step and an action plan should also be developed. All very simple and the explanation of each step is discussed in detail so there is no doubt in time to act.

The entire plan is thought from 4 points: client, values of customers, channel that the client uses to buy, and customer relationships. These items were already discussed in Canvas.

A simpler way of thinking a strategic plan can be used step by step below:

1 Set the Goals by Theme / Area;

Example:

Subject	Objective	Performance index	Results						
			Current	Projected					
			1999	2000	2001	2002	2003	2004	
Financial economic results	Operating margin of 13.5%	MO=(LL./RL.) X 100	8,2	8,32	9,68	10,99	12,27	12,51	
Market share	Grow 6% annually in Tachimied plan	BG = (No. of entries from BG / total inhabitants) x 100	25,15	26,65	28,25	29,95	31,75	33,65	
	Grow 3% annually the n° of attentions	(Number of subscribers / total inhabitants) x100	9,63	10,20	10,82	11,46	12,15	12,88	
Quality	Achieve 97% customer satisfaction	Customer satisfaction index	92	93	94	95	96	97	
	Reach 84% of employee satisfaction	Employee satisfaction index	77	80	81	82	83	84	

Figure 14: Objectives (Vasconcelos and Pagnoncelli, 2001, pg. 366).

2. Define what to do to achieve each goal:

Example:

<u>Objective 1:</u> economic / financial result: it has an operating margin of 13.5%

<u>Strategies:</u>

Create a differential service;

Increase competitiveness and enhance the services;

Etc ...

3 Set the action plan (how to do) for each strategy:

Example:

<u>Objective 1:</u> economic / financial result: it has an operating margin of 13.5%

<u>Strategies:</u>

Create a differential service;

<u>Action plan:</u>

- Develop an application for the customer to schedule the service;

- Provide a customer care agenda in the company's website so that he/she can schedule the service quickly with just one click;

- Etc...

Once the strategic plan has been designed, the next step is taking action: terminate the product and put it on the market following the pre-set plan. However, it has to be done before designing the financial spreadsheet for monitoring investments.

To start, write your ideas here.

OBJECTIVES

Theme	Goal	Performance indicator	Results					
			Current	Planned				
			2014	2015	2016	2017	2018	2019

STRATEGIES:

Objective 01:
_____
_____
_____

_____
_____
_____

Objective 02:
_____
_____
_____
_____
_____

Objective 03:

_____
_____
_____

_____
_____
_____

Objective 04:

_____
_____
_____

_____
_____
_____

Objective 05:

_____
_____
_____

_____
_____
_____

ACTION PLAN:

Objective 01:

Strategy:

Action plan:

Objective 02:

Strategy:

Action plan:

Objective 03:

Strategy:

Action plan:

Objective 04:

Strategy:

Action plan:

Objective 05:

Strategy:

Action plan:

8.2 Financial Guidance

This is when the entrepreneur assesses the effective costs and investments in the business. How much have you invested? How much is your product real cost? Are you writing everything down on paper?

The following is a template spreadsheet to control investments:

INVESTMENTS

INVESTED ITEMS:	MONTHS			
	1	2	3	4
Getting Around:				
Fuel				
Tolls				
Food				
Education and training:				
Courses				
Reading material				
Forums and Events				
Minimum Viable Product:				
Workforce				
Raw Material				
Communication:				
Business card				
Website				
Product Promotion				
Sales				
Partners:				

	MONTHS			
Partner hour work 01				
Partner hour work 02				
TOTAL:				

THIRD PARTIES INVESTMENTS

	MONTHS			
INVESTED ITEMS:	1	2	3	4
Stationery:				
Sulfite				
Post it				
Pens				
Meeting Room:				
Co-working Space				
Work time:				
Mentor 01				
Mentor 02				
TOTAL:				

TOTAL INVESTMENTS	

In these two template spreadsheets, detail what the entrepreneur and third parties (if any) have invested so far. Rows can contain more or less information, according to what you need to invest in each segment or product.

But the most important is to identify how much every entrepreneur invested in working hours. How much is your time worth in work? After all, if I were in a company - as an employee -that would be the salary.

It is usually at this time that the entrepreneur realizes how much it has really invested in the idea. I have seen cases of startups who dropped out of receiving angel investment because the offered value was much lower than the own partners that had already invested in work time. And, this is the main investment of the business: the entrepreneur is the one who makes the difference in a startup and it is the more "expensive" business asset.

Anyway, at the end you sum up all that has been invested, until that day. All the entrepreneur "spent" is investment because there was still no product being sold.

To start, write your ideas here.

INVESTMENTS

INVESTED ITEMS:	MONTHS			
	1	2	3	4

	MONTHS			
Total:				

The next step is to make a prediction of inputs and outputs. For this we use a simple template spreadsheet for cash flow, as in the example for cash flow on page 119.

In the spreadsheet, the entrepreneur should identify the input forecasts, according to the stipulated goals and all predictions of the outputs, including those that do not yet exist. This means a startup that uses the one of the partners house as a working basis, usually does not pay rent, water, electricity, internet access; however, these items are part of the company's cost and need to be accounted for there to be an actual calculation of return.

Thus, include these "unpaid costs" by the startup in this spreadsheet to effectively obtain how much the return will be at the end of the acceleration process with the following calculation:

(Total Balance at the end of four months - Total investment) / Total investment =% return in the period

It is yet a simplistic mathematical operation, comparing to what the investors and the stock market do; even though, it is enough to know "how much" beforehand and if the business could pay off.

There are instances in which the return was only possible without counting the costs of rent, water, electricity, telephone, etc. When this happens, everything needs to be revised, even if it is a feasible idea or not. After all no one wants to leave losses, not even for yourself.

Following is the presentation of results of the return in investment, the entrepreneur decides whether to actually sell his/her product on the market, or if the expected return is little and it needs to be rethought.

Print the complete worksheet of page 107 directly on the website:
www.sandraelisabeth.com.br/books/

Cash Flow Example

CASH FLOW	Previous TOTAL		Month 1 TOTAL		Month 2 TOTAL		TOTAL	
INPUTS	Forecasted	Outcome	Forecasted	Outcome	Forecasted	Outcome	Forecasted	Outcome
Revenues	$0	$0	$0	$0	$0	$0	$0	$0
							$0	$0
							$0	$0
Investments	$0	$0	$0	$0	$0	$0	$0	$0
Company (Shareholders-Founders)							$0	$0
Angel investors/Accelerators							$0	$0
TOTAL INPUTS	$0	$0	$0	$0	$0	$0	$0	$0

	TOTAL		TOTAL		TOTAL		TOTAL	
OUTPUTS	Forecasted	Outcome	Forecasted	Outcome	Forecasted	Outcome	Forecasted	Outcome
Utility Expenses	$0	$0	$0	$0	$0	$0	$0	$0
Rent							$0	$0
Taxes on utilities							$0	$0
Water							$0	$0
Energy							$0	$0
Communications							$0	$0
Equipments	$0	$0	$0	$0	$0	$0	$0	$0
Furniture							$0	$0
Office equipment							$0	$0
Remodeling expenses							$0	$0
Cleaning supplies and Office	$0	$0	$0	$0	$0	$0	$0	$0
Office supplies							$0	$0
Cleaning supplies							$0	$0
Printing supplies							$0	$0
Other supplies							$0	$0
Marketing and communication	$0	$0	$0	$0	$0	$0	$0	$0
Presentation cards							$0	$0
Visual communication							$0	$0
Events and meetings							$0	$0
Webpage and domain registration							$0	$0
Law and accounting	$0	$0	$0	$0	$0	$0	$0	$0
Accounting expenses							$0	$0
Company registration							$0	$0
Knowledge	$0	$0	$0	$0	$0	$0	$0	$0
Magazine subscriptions							$0	$0
Books							$0	$0
Production costs	$0	$0	$0	$0	$0	$0	$0	$0
Raw materials 1							$0	$0
Raw materials 2							$0	$0
TAXES - X% ON INPUT AVERAGE		[1]		$0		$0		$0
Withdrawal of founders							$0	$0
TOTAL OUTPUTS	$0	$0	$0	$0	$0	$0	$0	$0

INVESTMENT	Forecasted	Outcome	Forecasted	Outcome	Forecasted	Outcome		
							$0	$0
							$0	$0
							$0	$0
							$0	$0
TOTAL INVESTMENTS	$0	$0	$0	$0	$0	$0	$0	$0
MONTHLY BALANCE	$0	$0	$0	$0	$0	$0	$0	$0
TOTAL BALANCE	$0	$0	$0	$0	$0	$0	$0	$0

When the choice is to place the product on the market, it is necessary to check if the product is ready and if it will meet what was discussed during the first two months.

WRITE HERE YOUR INITIAL IDEAS:

$$\frac{(\text{Total balance at the end of four months} - \text{Total investment})}{(\text{Total investment})} = \underline{\hspace{2cm}} \% \text{ Return}$$

8.3 Monitoring

At the end of setting strategies , the entrepreneur will check for one last time the minimum viable product, measures if it is in accordance with the planned business model, if the sales channels are ready to work and how is the channel relationship with the client.

In some cases, this is when the acceleration process stops. This is because the entrepreneur ends up needing more time to put his/her MVP in the market. Some postpone the idealized product for too much and ends up being obsolete or is replaced by a competitor that previously did not exist.

And it is to this point that we draw attention: the process proposed here is 6 months in order for that soon the entrepreneur know if your product is or is not accepted by the chosen audience and to make necessary changes to please the customer.

We have seen cases of startups that would establish specific dates and are unable to have the MVP ready for testing.

Anyway, those who can place their products on the market, concluding the **setting strategies** , they quickly realize what is necessary to gain scalability and grow.

WRITE HERE YOUR INITIAL IDEAS:

How is your minimum viable product?

What is lacking for it to be ready for the market?

Put a deadline to start sales:

Monitor

mo.ni.to.r

(Monitor +ing [2]) vtd Monitorized.

Monitor

mo.ni.to.ri.zing

(Monitor + izing) vtd **1** follow up and evaluate data provided by electrical apparatus.**2** control through monitoring.

Now we need to keep track of what will happen with this product on the market. It's time to start the sales stage, that is, the time to get feedback from customers.

And it is at this stage that we have more resistance and drop outs. This is to say, not all entrepreneurs can take the idea from paper to the market to test. Much of it remains in the planning stage, but not in the action plan.

The entrepreneur's role is to make the adjustments at a minimum viable product by the feedbacks happened during sales.

For a lot of people is difficult to understand that a company will never, in situations of competition and normal markets, have 100% of the market and avoid hearing "no" from any customer. Usually when startups hear the first "no", they determine to change everything and go back to planning, even though before listening to some "sins".

9.1 Return Over Investment Forecast (ROI Forecast)

With sales going on, it is the time to measure if what is being billed is enough to cover costs, and how this revenue is in return of what was invested.

In some cases, it turns out that the business only pays when it's under a large scale, due to the very high fixed costs. In others, the variable cost is the problem that makes the business not profitable because the end user does not accept to pay the price of product costs.

This second case usually happens, and it is not exactly understood what the values of this target audience search. These are indicators of what is to be pivoted, how to change and which way to go.

The calculation for the ROI Startup is simple:

(Revenue - Total investment) / Total investment =% return in the period

We know this is a very simplistic calculation to speak on ROI. But if it is not earned in six months at least 20% of the investment according to the MVP, something may be wrong and you will need to recheck the Business Model and pivot.

9.2 Seek for necessary mentors

Before pivoting, it is important that the entrepreneur shares their difficulties with other entrepreneurs and mentor. This is the sharing with others who have gone through this initial phase and had success.

These conversations, that can also make you pivot a business or stop it, are important for the startup .

It is not an easy decision. So forth, it is essential to figure the mentor who can understand the market, the needs and guide the entrepreneur. His role is not to find out what, how and why to do it as consultants do, but to guide.

The entrepreneur needs to understand the reasons that led him to make a decision, not only being able to simply handle it. Remember, you are getting started and trying to know everything, and have everything on hand. If at this point you can't decide, then you should better think of another business.

9.3 Validation of the Business Model and the MVP

When sales take place and the business develops sustainably, the Business Model is shown and the MVP is validated. Now you need to take the second sustainable step and continue to grow organically, or receive investment of an Angel Investor.

We know that this sustainable growth is through entrepreneurs´ hard work for over six months. You can't always achieve the expected results: the project absolute success. But it is possible to identify another important point: do not invest in something that will not bring you any return.

Only after the MVP validation is that startups should seek Investor Angels or Venture Capital (depending on the project). It is interesting that some of the startups we know, and that had their MVP validated wouldn't like to have investors. They prefer to grow organically, at their pace and avoid having the need to be accountable to a third party.

Result
re.sul.ts

sm (part of result) **1** Action or effect of an outcome.**2** What comes out of something; Consequently, end product; Finally, term.**3** deliberation, decision.**4** Gain, profit. Mat **5** Conclusion of a mathematical operation. Give a result of: producing cause. Have resulted: become unusable or no effect.

The final result of this book is not for companies to receive a large investment, and that all businesses will become the "next Facebook". In fact, we hope this method minimizes the risks of the entrepreneur in his venture. That is, to prove if the original idea is feasible or not. If it has market and its current dimension.

Each Startup that has gone through this process had its particular success. Some have concluded that the personal investment on time and resources would not be worth the results they achieved.

Others realized they had great potential for growth, but not scale; i.e. they have great sales, enough for the members to maintain the business, but it will not be the "pupil of the eye" for large investors.

And there are those who give up before they even start. The first analysis realizes that the market would not be willing to buy the solution, not the original shape. It would be necessary to focus on the opportunity and draw another solution to it, which some entrepreneurs found hard to do.

So at the end of all, this method has helped entrepreneurs to avoid using the entire investment feature that allowed everyone to have the chance to pivot products / services, and restart the market validation process. It even gave the chance to use this feature to settle in the market and continue with the company sustainable growth.

We assure the proposed model will give any project a lot of success, but also hard work. It is your choice to test your idea.

WRITE HERE YOUR FINAL IDEAS:

What is the feedback from your customers about your product?

Is it worth continuing to invest this way? Or should you give yourself the chance to pivot?

What was the return on investment you had so far?

There are several ways for the entrepreneur to start a business in Brazil. Here we will present the forms of "lean startup" for this to happen, that is, the least costly as possible.

11.1 Support entities for entrepreneurs

Brazil possesses some entities that support the development of new business. We would like to mention some them as follows:

-SEBRAE

-APEX

-National Confederation of Industry (CNI by its initials in Potuguese)

-Trade Associations

Following there is a brief explanation of what they do and how they help .

11.1.1 SEBRAE [2]

The Brazilian Service of Support for Micro and Small Enterprises (SEBRAE) is a private non-profit entity. It is a training and promoting development office, created to provide support to small businesses across the country.

SEBRAE is a training and promoting development agency, but it is not a financial institution, so it does not lend money. It articulates (together with banks, credit unions and microfinance institutions) the development of appropriate financial products to the segment's needs. It also advises entrepreneurs that need access to credit, in fact, a business improvement tool.

[2] Informações coletadas no site da entidade: www.sebrae.com.br

SEBRAE meets those who are willing in starting their own business, those who already have their own business and want to expand their results, and also those seeking their business formalization.

SEBRAE operates in entrepreneurship education, training entrepreneurs and businessmen; in articulation of public policies that create a more favorable legal environment, access to new markets, access to technology and innovation, and guidance to access financial services.

11.1.2 APEX-Brazil [3]

The Brazilian Agency for Export and Investment Promotion (Apex-Brazil) works to promote Brazilian products and services abroad and attract foreign investment in strategic sectors of the Brazilian economy.

The Agency conducts diversified trade promotion aimed at promoting exports and value the Brazilian products and services abroad, as prospective and trade missions, business meetings, supporting the participation of Brazilian companies in major international affairs, foreign buyers, trainers and analyzers´ visits, to know the Brazilian productive structure and other business platforms that also aim to strengthen the Brazilian brand.

Apex-Brazil coordinates the efforts of attracting foreign direct investment (FDI) to Brazil focusing on strategic sectors for the development of competitiveness of Brazilian companies and the country.

It acts in many ways to promote the competitiveness of Brazilian companies in their internationalization processes. Among the services offered by this agency are market intelligence, business qualification, strategies for internationalization, business promotion and image, and investment attraction.

11.1.3 National Confederation of Industry (CNI) [4]

---

[3] Informações coletadas no site da entidade: www.apexbrasil.com.br
[4] Informações coletadas no site da entidade: www.portaldaindustria.com.br/cni

CNI is the voice of the Brazilian industry. The organization actively works to defend the interests of the productive sector, having as its mission to defend and represent the industry.

The CNI operates in the following areas: competitiveness, membership development, economy, infrastructure, innovation, internationalization, laws and regulations, environment and sustainability, small businesses, industrial policy and intellectual property.

CNI includes the industrial area, which is the base of the industry's representation system in Brazil, and it has 27 federations that bring together more than 1,250 unions and 350,000 companies. Together, these institutions represent the interests of the productive sector in search of a business environment conducive to the country sustainable development.

11.1.4 National Confederation of Commerce (CNC) [5]

The National Confederation of Trade in Goods, Services and Tourism is a labor union representing the rights and interests of nearly five million Brazilian entrepreneurs in the commercial sector. Together, these categories account about 1/4 of the Gross Domestic Product (GDP) and generate about 16 million direct and formal jobs.

The CNC ensures the interests and industry development in jurisdiction and advisory bodies, in Brazil and worldwide. In these organisms, it contributes to the decisions and formulation of guidelines for economic, administrative, social and environmental policies.

However, the performance of CNC goes beyond defending the interests of these segments. The Confederation manages also one of the world's social systems development - the Social Service of Commerce (SESC), working in the areas of education, health, culture and leisure, and the National Service for Commercial Education (SENAC), the main agent-oriented professional education for the sector of trade in goods, services and tourism.

---

[5] Informações coletadas no site da entidade: www.cnc.org.br

11.2 Starting your business the "lean startup" way

After your idea or project has been validated, it is time to turn "all this" into the real deal. For this, you need a CNPJ (National Register of Legal Entities) which is the register administered by the Federal Revenue of Brazil that records the registration information of legal entities and some that are not characterized as such.

Beyond being an identification document for the Brazilian Federal Internal Revenue Service, the CNPJ is used for opening legal bank accounts, financing, and preparation of contracts, and for many other purposes.

According to the Brazilian Federal Internal Revenue Service to request a CNPJ is necessary to submit the following documents:

a) FCPJ -. Registration Form of Legal Entities, which is filled directly on the website of the Federal Revenue of Brazil (RFB) http://www.receita. fazenda.gov.br, through the Web Application Collection. The FCPJ should be accompanied by the QSA (for companies);

b) Table Members and Administrators (QSA);

c) File specifies, of interest to the covenant agency, and

d) Basic Document CNPJ Entry (DBE) or Transmission Protocol as the models in Annexes I and II of IN RFB 1183, to August 19, 2011.

And if you are not Brazilian, you still need to submit the Brazilian visa at the consulate along with other documents.

It might be hard to understand, but our advice is to look for an accounting office and request for the counter to perform all the necessary procedures.

It is really important to understand the flow of the start-up process in Brazil, which currently follows this model, according to the Portal of Citizenship and Justice of the Federal Government:

The opening process begins with the business name search on the trade board and simultaneously with the address search and the possible activity desired there, done at the city hall.

After approval of the initial questions, the next step is to prepare the act of registration or incorporation of the company and sign the lease, if applicable. These measures prevent demands being made by registries and legalization, which delay the company's initial public offering. Also places where investments are made in, may not work.

Then, one must realize the company registration in the Commercial Board or notary registration in the National Register of Legal Entities (CNPJ) and goes to the business license. Once all these procedures are performed, the company can now operate legally.

We would visually have the following outline:

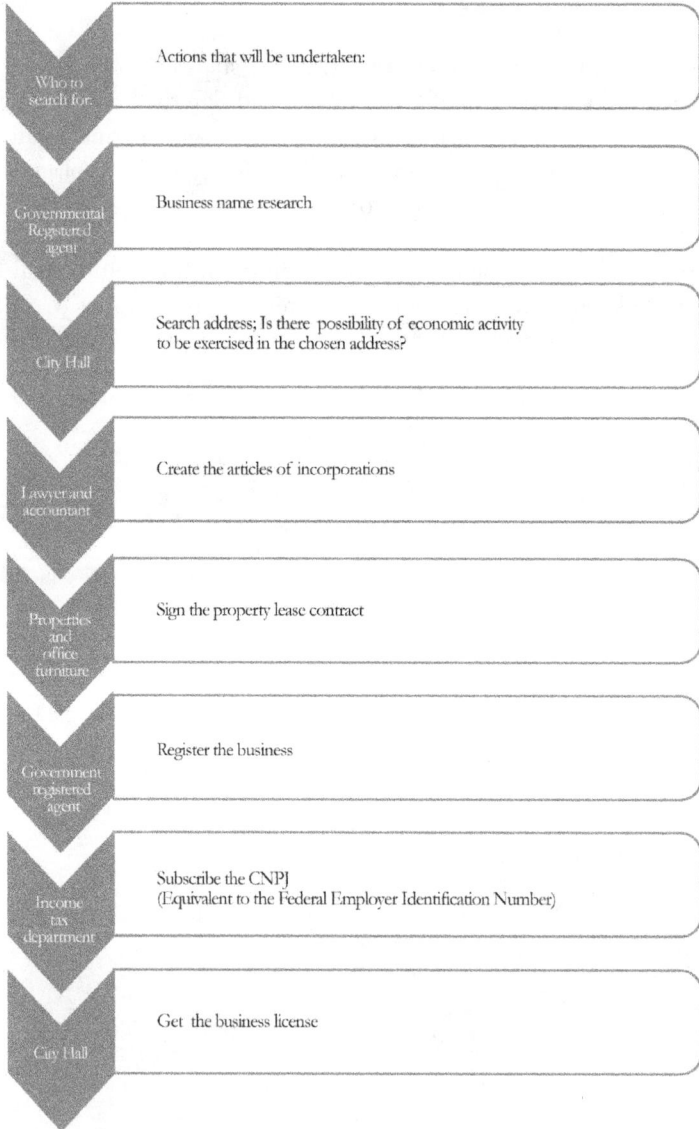

Stage	Action
Who to search for:	Actions that will be undertaken:
Governmental Registered agent	Business name research
City Hall	Search address; Is there possibility of economic activity to be exercised in the chosen address?
Lawyer and accountant	Create the articles of incorporations
Properties and office furniture	Sign the property lease contract
Government registered agent	Register the business
Income tax department	Subscribe the CNPJ (Equivalent to the Federal Employer Identification Number)
City Hall	Get the business license

The quickest and the cheapest way to start a new business is formally becoming MEI (Micro Individual Entrepreneur). In this case the formalization is made free of charge via the Internet at www.portaldoempreendedor.gov.br address.

After the registration, the inscription with the Commercial Registry, the CNPJ, Social Security and Operation Interim Permit are obtained immediately generating a single document that is the Certificate of Individual Micro entrepreneur condition - CCMEI.

The Micro-entrepreneur has no fees for registering the company. It should nearly pay 5% of the minimum wage INSS; $ 5 for ISS (Service Providers) and R$ 1 ICMS (Trade and Industry). The values are collected together by a carnet issued exclusively in the Portal of Entrepreneur and the maturity of the tax is by the 20th of each month.

But attention:

-The MEI can only win $ 5,000.00 (five thousand dollars) per month or R $ 60,000.00 (sixty thousand dollars) per year.

-To be characterized as MEI, the entrepreneur can't issue invoices only for a client, as this features a bond of employment between MEI and the client; with the client in this case to answer a process in the labor courts and run the risk of paying fines and compensation to the entrepreneur due to "irregular work".

11 .3 What is the best way?

The Brazilian bureaucracy is such that some multinational companies end up hiring outsourced accounting firms to help in this process. And if these "giants" who are long in the market will need this help, for whom this is getting more confusing and complicated yet.

The trick is always to look for a good accountant to help you in starting a formal business, or as it is known in Brazil: starting a business.

The role of the accounting office goes beyond determining taxes and accounting for days. He contributes to all areas of the company, often performing advisory and consulting activities. Some companies also offer audit services and foreign investment in Brazil.

And generally the initial consulting, to provide necessary information documents, best business model (MEI, LTD, Single, etc.) is free.

It is important to talk to these professionals because they know the "ways of the stones". They know when you will need CETESB (Environmental Company of the State of São Paulo - State Government agency responsible for the control, supervision, monitoring and licensing of pollution-generating activities, with the fundamental concern to preserve and restore the quality of water, air and soil). They also know if the address you chose to start your venture is allowed to have established companies. Finally, they know all the details of the federal, state and local laws regarding the opening of a CNPJ.

They make no mistake, beyond existing laws, depending on the NCEA (National Classification of Economic Activities) of your venture there will still be many other rules you need to follow, as INMETRO (National Institute of Metrology, Standardization and Industrial Quality), Health Surveillance, among others.

So as not to miss the best to talk to someone specialized. In this case, we always recommend a good accountant.

ACS, Zoltan J.; AMORÓS, José Ernesto (2008): Introduction: The Startup Process. Estudios de Economía. Vol. 35 - N° 2. Pags 121-138.

ANTUNES, J.;...[et al.], (2008) Sistemas de produção: conceitos e práticas para o projeto e gestão de produção enxuta. Porto alegre: Bookman.

BRIGIDI, Gabriel Mombach (2009) Criação de conhecimento em Empresas Start-up de alta tecnologia. Universidade Federal do Rio Grande do Sul, Escola de Administração, Programa de Pós Graduação em Administração – Mestrado em Administração.

CALADO, R. D. (2006) Aplicação de Conceitos da Manufatura Enxuta no Processo de Injeção e Tampografia de Peças Plásticas. Dissertação de mestrado acadêmico apresentada à comissão de Pós Graduação da Faculdade de Engenharia Mecânica, como requisito para a obtenção do título de Mestre em Engenharia Mecânica. Unicamp, Campinas, SP.

CALADO, R. D; CALARGE, F. A.; BATOCCHIO, (2010) Antônio; Método de diagnóstico empresarial - MDE: melhorias do gerenciamento da capacidade e otimização dos processos, 09/2010, XVIII Simpósio Internacional de Engenharia Automotiva (SIMEA),Vol. cd, pp.1-8, São Paulo, SP, Brasil.

CALADO, R. D., LIMA, P. C. (2003) A Aplicação da metodologia de Célula de manufatura na Solução de Risco de Acidente: uma experiência em um fabricante de eletrodomésticos. In: II Congresso Brasileiro de Engenharia de Fabricação, São Paulo.

CAMPOS, V. F. (2004). Gerenciamento da rotina do trabalho do dia-a-dia. Nova Lima: INDG.

CARVALHO, M. M.; RABECHINI JUNIOR, R.. (2008) Construindo competências para gerenciar projetos: teorias e casos. São Paulo: Atlas.

CARVALHO, M.M., PALADINI, E. P. (2005). Gestão da qualidade: teoria e casos. Rio de Janeiro: Elsevier.

CHAVES, N. M. D. (2006) Caderno de campo das equipes de melhoria contínua. Nova Lima: INDG.

CHAVES, N. M. D. (2005). Soluções em Equipe. Nova Lima: INDG.

CHRISTOPHER, M. (2007). Logística e Gerenciamento da Cadeia de Suprimentos: criando redes que agregam valor. São Paulo: Thomson Learning.

CORRÊA, H. L. (2010). Gestão de redes de suprimentos: integrando cadeias de suprimentos no mundo globalizado. São Paulo: Atlas, 2010

CORRÊA, H. L.; CORRÊA,C.A. (2007). Administração de Produção e Operações. São Paulo: Atlas.

DAILEY, K. W. (2003) The Lean Manufacturing Pocket Handbook. USA: DW Publishing Co.

DAUGHERTY, P. J., PITTMAN, P.H. (1995). Utilization of time-based strategies Creating distribution flexibility/responsiveness. International Journal of Operations & Production Management, Vol. 15, No. 2, pp. 54-60.

FELD, W.M. (2000). Lean manufacturing: tools, techniques, and how to use them. CRC.

GAITHER, N.; FRAIZER,G. (2007). Administração da Produção e Operações. São Paulo: Thomson Learning.

GEM – GLOBAL ENTREPRENEURSHIP MONITOR. (2011) Global Report.

HERRMANN, Bjoern Lasse (2011). Estudo mapeia genoma das startups: Em um levantamento feito com 12 mil empresas iniciantes do Vale do Silício, pesquisadores americanos apontam as razões do sucesso e do fracasso de uma startup. Vale do Silício nos Estados Unidos, Revista Pequenas Empresas & Grandes Negócios, Outubro de 2011. Entrevista a Thomaz Gomes. Disponível em http://revistapegn.globo.com/ Revista/Common/0,,EMI270599-17156,00-ESTUDO+MAPEIA+GENOMA+DAS+STA RTUPS.html. Acessado em 25 de novembro de 2013.

HART, Mark A. (2012) The Lean Startup: How Today's Entrepreneurs Use Continuous Innovation to Create Radically Successful Businesses. The Journal of Product Innovation Management, 29(3):506–510.

IUDÍCIBUS, Sérgio de e MARION, José Carlos. Curso de contabilidade para não contadores. 3. Ed. São Paulo: Atlas, 2000.

JACOBS, F. R.(2009). Administração da Produção e de Operações: o essencial. São Paulo: Saraiva.

KAPLAN, R. S.; NORTON, D. P. (1997). A estratégia em ação: balanced scorecard. Rio de Janeiro: Elsevier.

KRAJEWSKI, L; RITZMAN, L.; MALIOTRA, M. (2009). Administração de produção e operações. 8 ed. São Paulo: Pearson Prentice Hall.

KOTLER, Philip e KELLER, Kevin L. (2006) Administração de Marketing. 12 ed – São Paulo: Pearson Prentice Hall.

KOTLER, Philip e KELLER, Kevin L. (2012) Administração de Marketing. 14 ed – São Paulo: Pearson Prentice Hall.

LIKER, J. K.; HOSEUS, M. (2009) A cultura Toyota: o modelo Toyota aplicado ao desenvolvimento de pessoas. Porto Alegre: Bookman.

LIKER, J. K.; Meier, D. (2007). O Modelo Toyota: manual de aplicação. Porto Alegre: Bookman.

LIKER, J. K.; Meier, D. (2008). O Talento Toyota: o modelo Toyota aplicado ao desenvolvimento de pessoas. Porto Alegre: Bookman.

MARTINS, P. G. (2005). Administração da Produção. São Paulo: Saraiva.

MIYAKE, D. I. (2008). Melhorando o processo: seis sigma e sistemas de produção Lean. In ROTONDARO,R. G.(coord.) Seis Sigma - Estratégia Gerencial para a Melhoria de Processos, Produtos e Serviços. São Paulo: Atlas.

MOREIRA, D. A. (2008). Administração da Produção e Operações. São Paulo: Cengage Learning.

MOREIRA, José Carlos (Coord.). Orçamento empresarial: manual de elaboração. 4. ed. São Paulo: Atlas, 1989.

MORGAN, James M. e LIKER, Jefrey K. (2008). Sistema Toyota de desenvolvimento de produto: integrando pessoas, processos e tecnologia. Porto Alegre: Bookman.

MURMAN E. et al (2002) Lean enterprise value: insights from MIT's Lean Aerospace Initiative. Palgrave, New York.

OHNO, Taiichi (1997). O sistema Toyota de produção: além da prosução em larga escala. São Paulo: Bookman Companhia.

OSTERWALDER, Alexander (2011). Inovação em modelos de negócios. Business Model Generation Rio de Janeiro, Alta Books.

OSTERWALDER, Alexander; PIGNEUR, Yves. (2010). Business Model Generation: A Handbook for Visionaries, Game Changers, and Challengers. John Wiley & Sons.

PORTAL DA CIDADANIA E JUSTIÇA DO GOVERNO FEDERAL. Documentação necessária para abertura de uma empresa. Disponível em www.brasil.gov.br/cidadania-e-justica/

PRADO, D. S.. (2004). Gerenciamento de portfólios, programas e projetos nas organizações. Belo Horizonte: INDG.

PRADO, D. S.. (2004). PERT/CPM. Belo Horizonte: INDG.

RECEITA FEDERAL. Cadastro Nacional de Pessoa Jurídica (CNPJ). Disponível em www.receita.fazenda.gov.br.

REICHHART, A., HOLWEG, M. (2007). Creating the customer-responsive supply chain: a reconciliation of concepts. International Journal of Operations & Production Management. Vol. 27, No. 11, pp. 1144-1172.

RIES, Eric. (2012). A Startup Enxuta: como os empreendedores atuais utilizam a inovação contínua para criar empresas extremamente bem-sucedidas. São Paulo: Lua de Papel.

ROTHER, M.; SHOOK, J. (2003). Aprendendo a enxergar: mapeando o fluxo de valor para agregar vlor e eliminar desperdício. São Paulo: Lean Institute Brasil.

SANTOS, J., et al. (2009) Otimizando a Produção com a Metodologia Lean. São Paulo: Leopardo.

SATOLO, E..G., CALARGE, F. C.; SALLES, J. A. A.; MAESTRELLI, N. C.; PAPA, M. C. O.; ABACKERLI, A. J. (2006). Uma análise sobre questões atuais do Sistema Lean Production: um estudo exploratório de um site internacional de discussões. In: Simpósio Internacional de Engenharia Automotiva, 14, São Paulo.

SHINGO, S. (1996). Sistema de Produção com Estoque Zero: o sistema Shingo para melhorias contínuas. Porto Alegre: Bookman, 1996.

SEBRAE – Serviço Brasileiro de Apoio as Micros e Pequenas Empresas. Disponível em www.sebrae.com.br. Acessado em 06 de novembro de 2013.

SLACK, N. , et al. (2008). Gerenciamento de Operações e de processos: princípios e práticas de impacto estratégico. Porto Alegre: Bookman.

SLACK, Nigel at all. (2009). Administração da Produção. 3 ed – São Paulo: Atlas.

STEVENSON, W. J. (2001). Administração das Operações de Produção. Rio de Janeiro: LTC.

VASCONCELOS FILHO, Paulo de, PAGNONCELLI, Dernizao (2001). Construindo estratégias para vencer. 9 ed. Rio de Janeiro: Elsevier.

WOMACK, J. and Jones, D. (1996), Lean Thinking, Simon & Shuster, New York.

WOMACK, J. P.; JONES, D.T.. (1998). A mentalidade enxuta nas empresas: elimine o desperdício e crie riqueza. Rio de Janeiro: Campus.

XAVIER, C. M. S. (2009). Gerenciamento de projetos: como definir e controlar o escopo do projeto. São Paulo: Saraiva.

www.ingramcontent.com/pod-product-compliance
Lightning Source LLC
Chambersburg PA
CBHW050510210326
41521CB00011B/2402

* 9 7 8 1 9 4 3 3 5 0 0 6 3 *